Days of Refugee
One of the World Known Lost Boys of Sudan

Nathaniel Chol Nyok

Foreword by U.S. Senator Johnny Isakson

Published by Waldorf Publishing
2140 Hall Johnson Road
#102-345
Grapevine, Texas 76051
www.WaldorfPublishing.com

Days of Refugee
One of the World Known
Lost Boys of Sudan

ISBN: 978-1-63587-161-6

Library of Congress Control Number: 2018933231

Copyright © 2018

All rights reserved. No part of this book may be reproduced or transmitted in any form or by any means whatsoever without express written permission from the author, except in the case of brief quotations embodied in critical articles and reviews. Please refer all pertinent questions to the publisher. All rights reserved. No part of this book may be reproduced or transmitted in any form or by any means, electronic or mechanical, including photocopying, recording, or by an information storage and retrieval system except by a reviewer who may quote brief passages in a review to be printed in a magazine or newspaper without permission in writing from the publisher.

"Cowardice asks the question: is it safe? Expediency asks the question: is it political? Vanity asks the question: is it popular? But conscience asks the question: is it right? And there comes a time when one must take a position that is neither safe, nor political, nor popular - but one must take it simply because it is right." --Dr. Martin L. King, Jr

Table of Contents

Dedication 1
Foreword 2
Prologue 4

PART ONE: A LOST BOY'S JOURNEY
    Chapter One: My Heritage 7
    Chapter Two: Journey to the Unknown 36
    Chapter Three: A New Beginning 48
    Chapter Four: Out of Ethiopia 64
    Chapter Five: Welcome to Kenya 77
    Chapter Six: The Call to Adventure 84

PART TWO: A JOURNEY TO A NEW LAND
    Chapter Seven: A Piece of Luck is
    Better Than Knowledge 91
    Chapter Eight: A New Land 100
    Chapter Nine: An Act of Peace 120
    Chapter Ten: From Refugee Camp to Hollywood 126
    Chapter Eleven: Possibility 140
    Chapter Twelve: Creating A Family 146
    Chapter Thirteen: Fields of Green 154

PART THREE: THE RETURN
    Chapter Fourteen: Crossing the Threshhold 163
    Chapter Fifteen: Family Reunion 171
    Chapter Sixteen: South Sudan's Independence Day 175
    Chapter Seventeen: The End and the Beginning 186
    Acknowledgements 194
    Author Bio 195

Dedication

Two phrases—honor our family even when I am not with you and you are a seed of the nation, were from my father Nyok Reech and Dr. John Garang, the founder of the Sudan Peoples' Liberation Movement/Army (SPLM/A) respectively. These two statements inspire the trajectory of my life every day. I dedicate this book "DAYS OF REFUGEE" to Dr. Garang and my father who are the sources of my pride and hope. I hope this book dedication soothes their expectations of me whenever they turn from their graves.

I also significantly and equally dedicate this book to my mother Kuer Kur, who through her breast milk, sweat and advice, fed me the value of community and humanity.

Furthermore, I dedicate this book to the entire leadership of SPLM/A especially Gen. Kuol Manyang Juuk and Gen. Salva Kiir Mayardit, who made sure that the dream of becoming a seed of the nation prevails.

Finally, I dearly salute my comrades, the Lost Boys of Sudan, whom we together, despite coming from distant and unfriendly villages, have built friendship, brotherhood and unbreakable camaraderie. This book is a dedication to our sufferings, courage and future.

Foreword

Nathaniel Nyok's story is as touching as it is incredible. His honest prose is true to his background, his character and his experiences as one of the "Lost Boys of Sudan." From living through war, starvation and loss, to being a "lost" refugee in America, Nathaniel found his way in a new country, even coming to help develop foreign policy for both South Sudan and the United States. His journey has taken him from Bor, South Sudan, to Washington, D.C., and even to Hollywood – advocating for education, political involvement and peace in South Sudan.

Nathaniel's perspective is realistic and invaluable, with a spirit of gratitude toward the many people who have helped him. His own hard work, positive attitude and sense of optimism have taken him far already, despite the harrowing conditions he has faced.

In this book, Nathaniel's story invites the reader to consider a number of themes. Readers will gain a new perspective on their position in the world, the outlook Americans share, and the way our government and we interact with our neighbors at home and abroad. However, to read it is to receive a firsthand account of a story that, as far-removed as it may seem for some, is still eminently relatable.

Nathaniel's dogged pursuit of his goals and education has inspired me in my own work as an elected official. His mission to help educate others led to the founding of his nonprofit organization Ambassadors for Change, which he leads along with his wife. I hope his story will inspire the reader to want to do more in the world, to work harder, and to strive for worthy and noble goals. Ultimately,

I hope readers of this amazing personal journey will be moved to join Nathaniel in opening his arms wider to help others even more.

--U.S. Senator Johnny Isakson, R-Ga.

Prologue

The world has classified us as "the Lost Boys of Sudan." *Lost.* Such a powerful word.

Yet this title "Lost Boys," with all of its implications of loss, has become, for me, a positive title, as these words have served to unify us, the Lost Boys of South Sudan. While so many of us have lost so much; our families, our homes and our childhoods to a brutal war, we have not lost everything. *we* have survived. In a way, perhaps we did lose a part of ourselves. Horror forever changes anyone. Yet, while we grapple daily with the ghosts of our past, we ourselves have not become phantoms, we are very much alive and I believe. I must believe. we have survived for a reason. We, who met in the refugee camps, arrived from many different villages, villages remote, distant, and even at conflict with each other. Yet, through the sameness of our position, of our loss, we drew together as a group, as one unified whole, working for the freedom and future success of our country.

I am constantly reminded of the book *New Friends* that our class read in the Pinyudo refugee camp, shared with us by Dr. John Garang. Like the children in this book, we, the Lost Boys, have become friends; we fight as one people, and as Dr. Garang instilled in us, we are the "seeds of the New Sudan," the hope of the people. That book and Dr. Garang's words have never left me as I strive to make a difference for my country.

I, who have been classified as *Lost*, live in the all too real reality of my present, haunted by the ghosts of my past but I stand; I fight, for myself, for my family, for what I still, even after the ravages of war, consider my home. I am but one of thousands whose stories of strength and pain parallel my own. We are, forever bound by the chains of our losses.

Through the mirror of each other, we recognize a link to a past forever altered; a heritage we continue to fight for in the new lands in which we find ourselves, a fight we forge in our minds and hearts. Yet we are connected by more than, these bonds of our past. We are united by a hope that enables us to survive and that drives us to succeed today. And while our shared heritage has forever united us, each of our stories, while painfully similar, are deeply personal. We each walked our own path, saw with our own eyes, felt our own loss, our own pain, and we hold our own hopes and dreams. I am Nathaniel Chol Nyok and this is my story.

PART ONE: A LOST BOY'S JOURNEY

"They looted everything, raped the women and shot the children. Afterward, they burned it all down."

~ John Garang

Chapter One: My Heritage

I came into this world in the same manner as everyone else in my Aboudit village in Bor, Jonglei State, South Sudan. I was born in a small conical hut, birthed by the help of a midwife. My mother believes I was born around 1979. I do not know my actual birthday, as birthdays are irrelevant to the Dinka. What matters is life and death. The Dinka did not know how to read and write and did not keep records. They based their history on events of times. My village, my people did not have schools. For example, in Dinka, a child born on a rainy day is Deng for a boy and Adeng for a girl; a child born in drought is Yak or Ayak. Beyond life and death, drought and rain, major wars and feats, what does not directly affect the lives of my people, the Dinka, a peaceful cattle herding people, is irrelevant. Instead of the marking of a day, I was celebrated and blessed as new capital for my family and community. I was the future of my family. Dinka traditionally buries umbilical cords, a tradition meant to draw children back to their birthplaces when they are grown. My umbilical cord was not buried. In a conversation with my mother during our precious reunion in 2009 after 22 years of separation, my umbilical cord, which burned with our house during the war, she said, was hanged in the ceiling as a symbol of prayer to God. Since we lost your older brother, we beseeched God to watch every step of your life within and outside our house with blessings. We prayed to not lose you by hanging your umblical cord closer to God in the ceiling, she said.

In Dinka tradition, birthdays do not matter, but naming matters, and every name has a meaning. Dinka do not name their children at birth. Instead, each child is named in a naming ceremony, held about one week after birth. On this occasion, the child is introduced to the community for the first time. After the birth of a child and until the naming ceremony, the baby is only seen by relatives and the midwife. Before entering to see the child, relatives must first wipe their feet on a piece of a broken mud pot at the entrance before seeing the baby.

In my naming ceremony, my family, as a tradition in the community dictated, donated a meal and celebrated with the whole community. Elderly men and women poured blessings on me as each of them held me in turns, and there I was named, Chol Nyok. I would not become Nathaniel, meaning "gift from God," until much later, after the horror. My family name, Chol, means compensation. My parents lost their firstborn, and they wanted God to bless me as a compensation for their first child. My father's name "Nyok," which is my family name, means "a sacrifice." Before conceiving with my dad, my grandparents sacrificed a lamb, and as a result, babadie, my father, was born. They named him Nyok, which means "sacrificial lamb" in Dinka.

Because of the war that ravaged my village and robbed me of my family, my home and my childhood, I often find myself thinking of my life in terms of "before" and "after," before with my family and after as a Lost Boy. It's a dangerous way to think. When my thoughts turn down this dark path that leads to nowhere, I immediately make an effort to center my thinking, to focus on the now. I realize that it is up to me to give my life meaning, and the memory of my father, his love and his sacrifice, helps me to achieve this difficult feat of the mind. While I was only about seven or eight years of age, when I last saw my father, I vividly recall the pride he had in our family's heritage and in our home, and witnessing this pride made me proud of him. Because of the importance my father attributed to our history, I learned to have pride in myself and in my people. The gift of these memories, my inheritance, is the treasure my father bestowed upon me. I believe that these early lessons planted the first seed of strength within my being, a seed that perhaps equipped me with the will and the strength to survive.

As it did when I was a child, the memory of my father's pride still has the power to make my chest swell with emotion. While my father attempted to impart to me the value of my heritage, and I admired him greatly, I did not gain a full understanding of the legacy of my people, until much later. Today, due to the teachings of my father and my own experiences, I am a proud Dinka Bor.

The name Dinka is the widely known classification of my people, but my people call themselves Jieng or Muonyjang, a loose translation for "people of the people or men among men," as the Jieng (Muonyjang) resisted colonialism and Arabization for centuries. My group, the Dinka Bor, which lives along the Southeast of the River Nile, is one of the many Dinka (Jieng) groups in South Sudan. Although the Dinka people share similar physical characteristics, possess similar customs, and speak the same language, their culture varies from subtribe to subtribe. The Dinka Bor has earned its illustriousness among the other Dinka groups for its unique prestigious culture and principled cultural beliefs; beliefs grounded in equality, justice, and fairness, as the Dinka Bor display a powerful consideration and concern for outside communities.

Traditionally, the Dinka Bor community comprises the sub-communities of Athooch, Gok, Hol, Nyarweng, and Twi. I belong to Athooch sub-community. Today, after the independence of South Sudan, the Dinka Bor community populates the Jonglei State with three counties, namely; Bor

County, Twi East County, and Duk County. Evidence of the value placed on equality is that Dinka Bor has no kingdoms. A chief, who is elected based on his reputation in the community, leads each sub-Dinka Bor community. On election day, candidates for chiefdoms form individual lines as villagers queue behind them to elect their chief in a simple majority.

As a reflection of his wealth and ability to care for himself and others, the chief has to build the largest family in the community, which demonstrates the chief's ability to provide for a large number of relatives as well as those in the community. The chiefdom is traditionally passed down through lineage to the chief's elder son; however, there are rare cases when a younger son can demonstrate more capable leadership abilities and an exception is made. The village can also choose a different chief from a different family if it loses trust in a ruling family, or if a particular ruling family serves the longest. The chief is the head of the community. He presides over the community's issues, settles disputes, maintains peace and order, helps in marriages, and acts as an inter-community link who represents the community in all relations with surrounding villages.

Known for its apt and ethical leadership abilities, many prominent leaders have risen out of the Dinka Bor community and incited positive change for their people. After Britain and Egypt, which, until 1946, ruled the northern and southern sections of Sudan as a condominium, granted power over southern Sudan to the Arab north. Black African Leaders from Southern Sudan, who were not consulted on this decision and who feared oppression by Arab-dominated government, decried the decision and asked for Southern Sudan self determination. Bullen Alier Bior, a Sudanese politician from Dinka Bor and one of the few South Sudanese delegates in the 1947 Juba Conference that addressed this growing strain, spoke vehemently for the rights of the southern Sudanese. William Garang Dut, Ajith Mayom Amel, Bul Koch, Ezra Majok Chol, and Johnson Malual Leek, who later became Dinka Bor representatives in Sudan's parliament, also campaigned for southern Sudan's autonomy. The tensions between the north and the south escalated when, in 1953, Britain and Egypt agreed to grant Sudan its independence in 1956, and the northern Arab government, which was about to receive power, defied many of the concessions agreed upon in the 1947 conference.

The growing animosities reached a head, when, in 1955, the Arab dominated Sudanese government, based in Khartoum, refused to pay military wages to the southern Sudanese soldiers stationed in Torit while they paid the Arab soldiers their wages. In the face of this injustice, the southern soldiers rose to mutiny. Other southern leaders joined forces to fight against the violations enacted upon the southern Sudanese in a movement that became known as the Anya nya, which means "Cobra poison," as the rebels fought to poison the northern tyranny out of southern Sudan. Dinka Bor politicians; Akuot Atem, Frederick Brian Magot, Paul Awel and Job Adier were among the top leadership of this 1955 rebel movement, and Joseph Lagu, a Bari, served as the leader of this movement. In 1967, a year that became known as *"Run e Bany,"* meaning "year of the chiefs," the Sudanese government, in an attempt to instill fear in the rebels, killed Dinka Bor chiefs for opposing the government. Rather than inciting fear and ending the rebellion as hoped, the murders of the chiefs served as fuel for the rebellion. The southern rebels fought even harder.

Shaken by the continued political upheaval, the Sudanese government sought to end the conflict. The Anya nya ultimately led to the 1972 Addis Ababa Agreement, a treaty that ended the Civil War in Sudan and granted self-government to southern Sudan, a government which became known as the Southern Sudan Autonomous Government (1972-1983). The Sudanese government further promised to share resources; water, minerals, and oil. Abel Alier, a notable Dinka Bor who first served as a judge, became the president of this Southern Sudan Autonomous Government and later, elected as the vice president of the Sudanese government. Even after the Second Sudanese Civil War, Alier remained active in his efforts in protecting the rights of the marginalized Christians and animists of Sudan and went on to stand as the chairman of the Electoral Commission during the 2011 South Sudan referendum.

Immediately following the Addis Ababa Agreement, however, the primarily Islamic Sudanese government disliked the freedoms granted by this treaty and did not keep its word. The Sudanese government continued to marginalize the south and infringe upon its resources. This growing sense of injustice exploded in 1983 when the Sudanese government dissolved the Southern Autonomous government and ordered all southern Sudanese forces to transfer to north Sudan. In an act that inflamed the outrage already felt by the south, President Jafari Nimeri issued a decree that declared Sharia law as the law for all of Sudan.

Led by two Dinka Bor army leaders, Captain Alier Nhial Mangardit and 2nd Leutanent Alier Ngong Jok, Bor non-commission officers Alier Deng Kuot (Alier-Acuetthon), Thiong Tat, Alfred Manyang Agok, Garang Ngang Abui, Ajak Thiong Kuai, and Garang Deng Yom (Deng-Amor) and under the official overall command of Kuanyin Bol Deng, another Dinka, the South Sudanese *105* army battalion stationed in Bor refused to transfer to north Sudan and the government attacked this battalion in Bor. The soldiers fought back in a mutiny. Makeer Jool Deng, from Bor, my community was killed. He was the first soldier to die and a symbol of liberation struggle that ensued. The government of Sudan, unaware of the plan, sent late Dr. John Garang to quell the mutiny. Instead, dissatisfied by the attempted Arabization of Sudan and the continued infractions on the shared resources, Dr. Garang, along with the late Martin Majier Gai, the late Arok Thon Arok, and many other prominent Dinka Bor men who held positions in the Sudanese government, defected from their posts to Ethiopia. They, along with other South Sudanese politicians founded the Sudan People's Liberation Movement (SPLM) and the Sudan People's Liberation Army (SPLA). Gai, a member of parliament in Sudan for Bor South, and Arok, a military general in the Sudanese army, deliberated with other South Sudanese politicians and elected Dr. Garang, a colonel in the Sudanese army and lecturer at the military academy in Khartoum, to serve as the commander-in-chief of the SPLA and chairman of SPLM. Garang, who, under the sponsorship of the Sudanese government, earned his doctoral degree in agricultural economics at Iowa State University and went on to graduate from Fort Benning Military Academy in Georgia, became the spokesman of the rebel movement. The SPLM/A, which consisted primarily of the Dinka and Nuer but included the joined forces of many south Sudanese tribes, waged a war of liberation against the government of Sudan to free the people of South Sudan and all the marginalized Sudanese. Their goal was to establish a democratic Sudan with the SPLM as the leaders of the south. Kuol Manyang Juuk, a German trained engineer and lecturer at Juba University, became a well-known army General of the Sudan People's Liberation Army and later, as a result of his efforts, became Governor of Jonglei State and South Sudan's Minister of Defense.

The list of Dinka men who fought for the rights of the southern Sudanese continues and is exhaustive, yet these pillars of the Dinka Bor community demonstrate the will of strong men, men amongst men, to strive for the justice and freedom of their people. I am proud to pursue and continue to build the road to freedom paved by the blood and efforts of these notable men, for I, too, am of the Jieng.

My father, as the life of the Dinka Bor centers on agriculture and animal husbandry, was a farmer and a pastoralist. I was very proud of the life of my father and desired to follow his footsteps. While my father, not considered extremely wealthy, had two wives and nine children, which demonstrated his ability to provide for his large, extended family, was viewed as relatively well off. I considered both my father's wives my mothers. My first mother, Adau Ayuen Chagai, is my father's first wife. My biological mother, Kuer Kur Dit, is his second wife. On my first mother's side, I have five brothers and one sister. I also have two biological brothers and a sister. My grandfather, Reech Akuok was married to four wives, so my extended family is large and consists of several uncles, mothers, cousins, nephews, and nieces.

I spent my childhood cared for and welcomed equally at both of my mothers' compounds; in fact, I was the favorite in both compounds, and I often helped them with the smaller tasks, such as gathering firewood, borrowing fire from a neighbor, and other small kitchen tasks. Because I was the eldest child to my biological mother, I helped her with my younger siblings. Both mothers imparted the histories of our people and shared communal stories that taught me the values of family, honesty, and independence. From my father, I learned the beginnings of how to be a man.

Yet, while fathers teach their sons how to be men, the women of my village play an integral role in a boy's initiation into manhood. As mothers, they teach their sons and daughters the importance of the community through training in daily tasks, and they transmit their values through their stories. I eagerly looked forward to the stories my mother told during chores and after dinner. Words held power to me, even then. Yet, like all boys, I could not wait to become a man.

In my village, once a son matures, after the age of six, he leaves his mother to go to cattle camp, the first initiation process into manhood, as the livelihood of the village centered on cattle. About age thirteen, and rarely, upon the request of the family, between ten and twelve, the boys in the cattle camp go through a month-long initiation process headed by the elder women that are the final initiators of boys into manhood, at which point the boys forever leave behind their childhood and the realm of the women and become men. During this initiation, the elder women perform sacred ceremonies to mark this final journey and offer final teachings on how to be a man. After this final rite of passage, if an elder boy, now a man, transgresses against the teachings of his community, he will stand as an abomination to the village. A Dinka Bor man, is expected to behave with integrity and honor.

I, like other boys, was insatiably curious about the initiation process; I couldn't wait until it was my turn to undergo this rite. I raced to watch my brother's initiation, eager to watch this mysterious passage into the realm of men. Like all of the younger boys, I knew not to stand too close to the older boys, who, full of hubris after their initiation and desperate to prove themselves men, would have beaten me had I stood too close. I smartly stood as a distant observer to my elder brother Chol Nyok's initiation. During the initiation rite, the boys travel with the elder women to a designated pen, a cattle stable, where each boy undergoes his own coming-of-age ceremony. When my brother was initiated with the other boys his age, our cattle stable was chosen to serve as a sanctuary for the initiates. I stood at a close distance from our family's pen and watched with a mixture of awe and envy as my brother emerged oily and proud with his hair shorn, chest jutted insolently forward, and neck adorned with the sacred cowrie shells - he was now a man and, to me, he seemed to stand taller. Staring at my brother, I felt a mixture of envy and awe - I could not wait to become a man.

Life in my village centers on cattle. In the mornings, I helped gather the cows for milking and led them to graze. After my chores were complete and while the cattle grazed, I, like the other children, played with what my environment provided; primarily, I played with clay. During grazing times, the searing heat sent the elders and children to pass their time in the shade. I would sit under the tree with the other children and mold clay into cows, the earth cool and soft in my hands. I enjoyed grabbing a lump of formless clay and molding it until, in my hands, it took the form of a favorite cow in the village, Yar, the great white cow, or Ayen, the cream cow. I would race, a young artist with his creation, to the grownups, who, to my excitement would exclaim, "What a beautiful cow. You could pay a dowry with that cow." My chest would swell with satisfaction. As the grownups kindly praised my handiwork, my fellow youth would snicker and tease my artistic endeavors, "Ah, Chol, you will never get a girl with that cow," or, "What part of the cow is that? Its dung?" Truly, my sad cows did bear a close resemblance to dung piles or, as I became more skilled, fat dogs, but the taunts did not faze me. Pleased by the elder's praise, I would run with the other boys to hide my expert crafts under the bushes to dry. The next day I would return with pride to claim my inspired creations.

In the evenings, after the day's chores were complete, I spent the remainder of my time playing games of hide and go seek, Adou, which is similar to American baseball, and Alueeth, which resembles football or rugby. We used a palm nut for a ball and played in a circular clearing. We didn't play to win; we played for fun. Although I was young, I remember, I was quite good at Adou—I would whack the ball beyond the circle every time. No one teased me during this game.

After the time for games, I returned to my father's compound to complete the evening with a meal of milk, cheese, and vegetables, followed by riddles and storytelling, my favorite time of day. I remember that I looked forward to my mother's stories, but, as I was young, I no longer remember these precious tales. They sadly fell through the kaleidoscope of childhood memory. I do, however, recall the cadence and warmth of my mother's voice and the sense of oneness her stories made me feel towards my brothers and sisters and my village. While I cannot recall the details of these stories, the impressions of my mother's words will always remain with me, sharp and clear.

Along with storytelling, my mother gave me the gift of song. Traditional singers were highly respected in my community, and my mother, who was renowned in the village for her beautiful voice, taught me to sing. I recall how much she loved to sing. She sang as she completed her daily tasks—raising my younger brothers and me. Since she had a special lullaby for each of us, she would hold me gently as she sang to me. Then she would smile and whisper, "That was your song." Her voice, vibrant and warm, wrapped about me like a blanket, and lifted and soothed me. As I grew older and helped with the chores, I sang with her. She taught me the lyrics to her songs, and how to harmonize with her. As I took care of my younger brothers, I repeated her lullabies to them. During planting times, my mother and father would sing together as we sowed the seeds. They would smile and laugh as I joined in their songs, my child voice in unison with their deep bass and smooth alto. Singing brought me pleasure, and it still does today, and like my mother, I am told that I am a good singer. When I was young, I took these times for granted, as the young do. They were a part of my daily experience, so I didn't realize how truly special they were. Now, after being apart from my mother for twenty-five years, the thought of her voice strikes a chord in me that transports me back to my childhood; to her warmth and her songs.

In her care, my mother taught me the importance of my elders, which held great importance in my community. She taught me that every woman is like my mother and every man is like my father and, therefore, deserving of respect, so I revered my elders and called all women "Mother" - "*Mama*," or "Auntie" - "*Wuai-wuai*" for paternal aunt or "*Malen*" for maternal aunt, and all men outside of the Father, "*Waa*" or "*Baba*," we called "Uncle" - *Walen* for paternal uncle or *Nornor* for maternal uncle. Equally important was a sense of community. My mother instructed me to call my peers *Wanmath*, brother, or *Nyankei*, sister, no matter who they were. My mother often said, "The degree of any relation is known, but proper salutations free souls."

While the elders are revered, the children are also highly esteemed by the village. My community profoundly believes in the African maxim, "it takes a village to raise a child," as children stand as the true capital of a society, as they are the foundation and continuity of a community. I was raised under this life philosophy. Because the entire community cared for the children, wrongs were also dealt with communally.

As a child, I was taught that a wrong was a wrong to everyone. A community member would beat a child for a wrong and then bring the child to his or her mother or father, where the child would be beaten for the same wrong again. There was no point in crying out for help, as the punished child would receive no sympathy from the elders. If anything, the crying child would be lectured on his or her wrong once more. Consequently, children quickly learned the boundaries of right and wrong and the importance of the community. Wrongs were not repeated.

Grandmothers, who were dearly respected by all, stood as an exception to this rule; they were the only saviors of children. If a child ran to a grandmother, he or she would be safe in her protection - if she so chose. Unfortunately, I didn't have a grandmother who could save me from the rare beatings I did earn. She died before I was born. As I feared the humiliation of punishment and desperately wanted to please my father - not to mention the fact that I lacked a savior, I tried my hardest to be good and avoid becoming one of the lucky recipients of our communal justice system.

Growing up in this communally based village, I was surrounded by people who worked together for the benefit of the whole. If a person needed a compound built, the community pitched in. Thanks would be offered with a feast and, for larger deeds, perhaps with the sacrifice of a cow or a goat. If there was a marriage celebration, everyone in the village came to take part.

Marriages are also the community's responsibility. To find a wife or a husband is never one person's responsibility. According to the Dinka Bor tradition, marriage is a unity between two people; two families; two communities; two villages; two clans; or sometimes even; two nations and and the husband and wife work together as co-owners of the family. Therefore, due to the importance of marriage, marriage is never left to the discretion of the marrying couple. My people arrange marriages, believing people grow into love. Experienced family and community members help to ensure that both the son and daughter marry into a respected family or community and that the inexperienced daughter marries a man worthy of her. Also, while a bride price enables a man to marry into a better family, if a man cannot afford a bride price and the bride's family deems him worthy, the community works collaboratively to gather the appropriate resources of cattle or goats to enable the man to marry.

While a Dinka woman is considered a child until she is married, after she is married, she becomes co-owner of her family, and, therefore, actively participates in major family decisions. If the husband dies, the wife inherits the children and all of his property and becomes the head of the family, to be followed by her children. If the community or her brothers-in-law meet, she is invited. If a wife's husband was a chief and there is no biological brother or grown son, the wife becomes the chief; this, however, was uncommon.

As a wife, a woman keeps her family name, and as a mother, she is given a chance to name some of her children after her ancestors, which ensures the genealogy of both the husband's and the wife's families. As the woman is important to her family in Dinka Bor society, it's tradition that when a girl is married and becomes pregnant, her husband and in-laws, during her pregnancy, take her to her biological family, who cares for her through her delivery until the baby is weaned. At weaning, she returns to her husband and his family with the special status of a mother within the family and the community.

For the same reason the community arranges marriages, an individual is unable to divorce a wife without family or community consent, as every wife belongs to the community. The wife serves her husband and community with her cooking, maintaining her home, and caring for the children, her own and those of the community, and through childbearing, she ensures the community's survival. Therefore, in keeping with the adage, "It's a woman who gives birth to a man; it's a woman who gives birth to a chief," women hold a significant position within the Dinka Bor community.

While the Dinka Bor did not have many enemies, I recall the words echoed by the elders and whispered by the children: "If you don't take care of yourself, if you don't sing a song, you will be abducted by the Murle." The Murle were notorious for their cattle raids and for their child abduction. The Khartoum government, well aware of these raids, did not view these thefts as a big concern. In fact, the government supplied the Murle with weapons; they wanted the southern tribes to prey upon themselves. The Southern tribes attacking each other served as the disunifying factor that benefited the government. As there were no schools, individual tribes did not understand the concept of national unity; they knew only tribal unity. Growing up, I did not realize there were tribes beyond the neighboring Dinka tribes. I thought our tribe was the world. The government exploitation of the southern tribes and their lack of education still strikes me in its sheer disregard of humanity.

To the Dinka, the name Murle, a whispered dread, meant fear. Every person in the village knew someone who had been abducted by the Murle. Some of the children I played with were kidnapped by this notorious clan. No one knew what happened to these children, but the two most likely rumors were that the Murle brainwashed them and turned them into Murle warriors, or they sold them into slavery. In response to this threat, all children were brought inside as soon as the sky turned to dusk. Even this precaution was not enough of a deterrent, as the Murle would sometimes sneak into the village and attack the family compounds. The village had to be on constant alert.

While the Murle received weapons from the government, with their constant raiding, they often ran low on ammunition, which made them more fearful. The Murle did not fire warning shots; to do so would waste precious ammunition. They knew only how to kill or be killed. During their dreaded attacks, Dinka Bor men would rush to defend the village, while the women, gathered the children and the elderly and ran with them into the jungle. In the chaos that often accompanied these raids, people scattered haphazardly, but the women grabbed the frightened children into their group and ushered them to the safety of the forest. I, like the other villagers, was taught to stay with a group, to join with the nearest group, and not to run alone. Once safely in the forest, the women would keep the children quiet until the men would enter the thicket and call for us, which signaled safety. As it was the man's duty to die for his village, the women were taught to be prepared that the men might not return. If a man died, the woman would have to step up to become the head of the family. She would raise the children, instill values, and provide for her family. Uncles and relatives would offer support, but the mother was the figurehead.

The synergy of their efforts ensured the survival of the community. The men served as the defenders of the village; the women, the protectors of the family.

In our community, we were also taught that strangers are God's messengers. As they come from other communities to see and tell about our kingdom. They must always be treated with kindness. Even with the threat of the Murle attack, every stranger that entered the village was to be accommodated, fed, protected, and treated with decency. I witnessed my mother treat every stranger from every walk of life with justice. Beyond the Murle tribe, the Dinka Bor did not have enemies. Although our enemy, a member of the Murle that enters our village in peace and wanted to stay according to the Dinka rule of hospitality, would be accepted.

Witnessing this close-knit interaction of people as I grew up, with the males and females working cooperatively together for the benefit of the community and with the communal care where everyone was either *Mama*, *Wuai-wuai*, *Malen*, *Walen*, *Nornor*, *Wanmath*, or *Nyankei*, I blissfully believed that everyone was my relative. However, 1983 marked the advent of the impending war and destruction of my village and the beginning of the end of my untroubled, youthful existence. I was about four years old.

The war entered my village one evening in a form of gunshots heard in the distance from Mading Bor, threatening bursts that reverberated sharply a common village warning, "Lion picks off an animal that strays from its herd."

The elder men's eyes clouded over with foreboding darkening skies. The women pulled their children closer. The younger men ran from house to house and to neighboring villages to find out the cause of this new unrest.

The following morning, military utility vehicles and pickup trucks with mounted guns skidded to a halt in our village. Arab soldiers, in green and camouflage uniform, exited the vehicles and proceeded to march ominously through the village, their guns hanging in a silent threat by their sides. They intimidated and interrogated my parents and neighbors as they besieged and ransacked their homes. Due to the language barrier, the Arab soldiers could not communicate with the villagers and a rudimentary sign language made up of gestures and grunts served as the medium of communication. The quiet, as the soldiers conducted their interrogations, settled thick and tangible upon the village. All lives, all movements halted. The women, warned by the men to remain silent and not draw attention, quietly guarded the young children.

As a child, I did not understand what was happening, and the stillness felt cold and strangling. Rather than succumb to the ominous pall that settled on the village, I pushed my fear from my mind. I, along with the other children, admired the strangers in their military uniforms - they were a novelty; we had never seen anything like them, and we were fascinated by their physical appearance. We naively followed the soldiers from home to home as they searched our village, and, perhaps sensing our innocence, they kindly welcomed our attentions.

On this occasion, the soldiers, finding nothing in the village, returned to the army barrack in Mading Bor, now Bor Town, the capital of Jonglei State, yet their portentous visit instilled a dread in the adults, who recalled Anyanya One and felt the threat of war seep unbidden into their minds. After the departure of the Arab soldiers, the childish adoration I felt for these soldiers was extinguished by the dread stamped upon the faces of the adults. My childlike intuition told me that these soldiers could not have intended us good. For the first time in my young life, I felt the sickening chill of fear.

Later, in the middle of that night, I awoke and saw with increasing trepidation about one hundred soldiers furtively leaving the village. Hearing them speak Dinka further augmented my confusion. My father, too, was awake. Sensing my agitation, he explained that the soldiers belonged to a unit led by Dr. John Garang and Kerubino Kwanyin Bol, who mutinied against Sudan's government in Mading Bor. The Arab soldiers had come to track them down because they had waged a war against the government.

My father stressed that had the Arab soldiers found Garang and Kerubino, it could have brought great disaster to our village. We could not bear the weight of their deaths. We could not betray these men. As my village holds all life as precious, blood spilled on the land could bring a curse to our land. The villagers ingeniously hid these rebel soldiers, burying Garang, Kerubino, and the other leaders in heaps of sorghum sticks and piles of manure and turning the soldiers into civilians.

I listened as my father explained the significance of the searches and these Dinka soldiers. The worry in his voice frightened me, but through the egocentric lens of childhood vision, the story seemed removed from me. I resumed my chores and games and continued with my childish life under my parents' protection, as did the other children of my village.

Only later did I understand the import of that episode, as it marked the juncture of the Sudan People's Liberation Movement (SPLM) and its military wing, the Sudan People's Liberation Army (SPLA), under the leadership of Dr. John Garang De Mabior. The Sudan People's Liberation Movement/Army later waged a war of liberation against the Sudanese government in Khartoum. The initiative brought pleasure to all South Sudanese who felt marginalized by the ruling Arab elites. The elders, however, remembered the bloodshed of the first Civil War, and knew that this war, too, would not be without cost. Nonetheless, after a few days passed uneventfully, the adults, like the children, returned to the routine of their daily lives. The veil of fear lifted. Life went on.

My father took care of me as his beloved first born and potential heir of his second family, yet he led our family with an egalitarian hand. I was not in any way different from his other children, each child was treasured, but since I was the oldest in his second family, I was important. My father, Nyok Reech Akuok, I estimate, was in his late sixties, and he knew he was aging and had to pass the responsibility of maintaining the family on to his children. My father began to groom me into a man, and I possessed a great admiration for my father and the wisdom of his lessons; lessons in work, fairness, and honor.

I learned one such lesson in fairness and honor when my uncle sued my father over a cow. During my aunt's marriage, my father was given a cow, but my uncle, another brother of my father, mistakenly thought that the cow was his. While the father and mother of the bride receive cows as a part of their daughter's bride price, occasionally, cows are also gifted to the bride's brothers. When there is only one cow given to the brothers, the eldest brother gets the cow, and when the next sister gets married, the cow is given to the second eldest brother, and so on down the line. Although it was my father's turn to receive a cow, his younger brother believed that my father wrongfully took his cow and brought the matter to chief's court.

The chief's court, presided over by the village chief, consists of a jury of elected people from the village who listen and decide on the outcome of the cases. Other villagers also come to listen. These bystanders often raise their hands and provide their opinions on the case, and sometimes their opinions are taken into consideration. My father took me with him to the community's court to help him bring the cow home, as he expected the court to rule in his favor, but to also introduce me to leadership and wisdom, as I listen to elders deliberating on cases before the court.

I walked confidently to the court with my father; I felt a

sense of maturity in being called upon to help him in this important matter. As my father and I listen to the deliberation in the under-the-tree courtroom, I grew bored of listening as I watched a group of children play a game of Alueeth. I bravely decided to join their game, but some of the boys did not take kindly to my interruption. The boys circled me, threatened to beat me and pushed me a few times before they allowed me to leave.

I returned to the court shamed and crying. Alarmed, my father asked me what happened. After narrating the story, I hung my head in dejection and muttered, "I wish I was an adult so that I could do what I wish." I wanted to fight those boys, to punish them for my humiliation, but I was younger and smaller. I was ashamed that I walked away and didn't fight back, as I wanted to make my father proud. My father did not add to my shame, and I will forever remember his response. He said, "Son, what is sudden is death, but aging takes forever. You will grow to do what you wish some day if God blesses you. However, remember not to let me down. Whether I am with you or not; always do the right thing to bring honor." Doing the right thing to bring honor was my family's common line, but his story was more than an offer of understanding and encouragement for my present situation. I believe that my father was giving me an indirect blessing, and his words follow me everyday. My father could not have known what the future held, yet his belief in my ability, his belief in me, gave me encouragement, and it still does. As I age every second, I think of my potential if God clears my way.

In early 1987, at about eight years, I forever left the domain of my mother and began my transition into the realm of my father as he primed me for manhood. My father sent me to the cattle camp, a giant island where cows are kept. For a few months, I stayed with my older brother Chol Nyok; my cousin, my father's sister's son, Thon Kuer; and my cousin, my father's brother's son Reech Nyok. They bore the responsibility of training me to become an independent and courageous man who could keep cattle and guard the community. I became the closest friend to Reech, as we were almost agemate, and we completed our daily tasks together.

Since our parents rarely lived in the cattle camp with us, the elder boys, usually ages twelve to eighteen, took care of the cattle. These boys, as they were being groomed to become men of the village, were left in charge in the camps. They were our leaders and mentors, and, therefore, our elders to be treated with respect. I was younger and new to the cattle camp and was not yet trusted with the older cows, so my job was to take care of the calves. I took them from place to place to graze and brought them back in the evening. I worked diligently to learn the way of the cattle. I wanted my father to be proud of me and undertook each of my responsibilities, even those less desirable duties reserved for the young novices like myself, with complete seriousness. I was a diligent collector of urine and cow dung.

As the Dinka life centered around cattle, the Dinka found use for everything connected to cows. The Dinka girls and newly-wed and unmarried men and women use cow urine to lighten their hair in a process of beautification, and in the villages, cow dung has many uses, but it is mainly used as manure. The cow dung also proved invaluable in the cattle camps, as it served as an effective insecticide. Reech and I would help collect the cow dung and spread it out to dry in the sun. Later, this dried cow dung would be gathered and burned in the evenings, and the ensuing cloud of smoke would hover protectively over the camp as a shield against insects. During working hours, we rubbed the ash of the burned cow dung into our bodies and into the bodies of the cows to stave off insects. The ash from the cow dung also functioned as toothpaste. The antiseptic quality of the ash from the cow dung cleaned our teeth and prevented infection.

Although I was young, I was expected to milk cows whenever there were no females, or older boys with experience in milking. These times horrified me even though I diligently tried, I wasn't very good at milking cows. I watched enviously as the girls and older boys would settle themselves next to a cow with ease and produce buckets of warm, fresh milk. While I attempted to approach the massive bodies of these uncooperative beasts with calm and confidence, the cows would sense my fear, and their twitchy agitation would send me dashing for safety, my task incomplete. When a stomp, snort, or tail swish didn't send me running, I still could not get the cow to release her milk because I lacked the experience.

My peers at the camp found amusement in my humiliation and would jeer, "Go home to your mother, *Yin cit Nya*," which means girlish, or "Go cook with your mother, *Wen e tik*." Which means Mama boy. All those expressions denoted weakness in a Dinka man, and this feeling got me so mortified. While milking cows was a woman's work that would never be expected of a man in our tradition, boys, until they reached the age of twelve, participated in this task. At age eight, I couldn't milk a cow; therefore, my peers pay me a strange ignominy. I felt embarrassed by the mockery, and the failure to reach under a huge cow to grab her udder. I was regretful that I couldn't complete this woman and young children's task correctly.

In the cattle camp, we mostly drank milk. Sometimes we ate meat, geese, tortoise, tilapia, eel, or the occasional antelope or topi, but as our work left little time for hunting, not too often. Occasionally, we took cattle to grazing land near villages, and from there, we brought maize and sorghum flour back to the camp. As we typically drank milk; morning, afternoon, and evening for months, the maize and sorghum flour was a longed-for delicacy at the cattle camp. We poured the sorghum flour into boiled water and roasted or boiled the maize, and after a few minutes of agonizing anticipation, we feasted greedily upon these delectable treats.

As cattle are precious to the Dinka and the people live to serve them, I was being trained to respect and continue in this great tradition. Because cattle require frequent attention, cows prevail at the center of the Dinka universe. People endure extreme weather in order to find them good grazing lands. In the dry season, children and adults trek hundreds of miles in search of fresh pastures. During the rainy season when there is flood and mud, cows are taken to the hilltops to save them from the waters. When the cattle rest or sleep, people lie along their sides to protect them from wild animals and raiders.

Because cattle are revered, the Dinka rarely killed or sold their cows. It's only on special occasions, such as marriages, memorial ceremonies, offerings to the gods, or initiation ceremonies that one or two cows were killed. Due to their importance, cows serve as insurance for the future; a single person or family could own hundreds of cows. Families with the wealth of cattle do not go poor for generations. However, cows do not just serve as Dinka's economic resources; they are friends and companions. They are a part of the Dinka family, and like children, have to be healthy and comfortable at all times.

To the Dinka, cattle are fascinating and great objects of admiration, and as I worked closely with the cattle, my fascination for them grew. Although all cattle are valued, the mixed colored cattle, especially the ones with white and black stripes or brown coloration, are highly revered. People name their children after such esteemed cattle and compose songs based on the inspiration of these magnificent beasts. The owners of these acclaimed creatures earn renown and become associated with the fame of their animals. Most people are nicknamed to bear the name of their highly valued cows. The colorful bulls are rarely sold or given way; they are kept for the purpose of prestige. On occasion, these honored bulls are given as a dowry to in-laws, and as thanks, a child born to such an honored couple would bear the name of the gifted bull. To me, learning to care for the cattle enabled me to become a part of the great cattle-keeping tradition in my village.

Life in the cattle camp was not all work — or entirely embarrassing. Cattle camp life delighted me. I felt free and grown. When the cattle grazed by the river, we often fished, and many of the other youths swam. Afraid to swim myself, I enviously watched as the other boys effortlessly crossed to the far shore. As I was young and new to the waters, I believed that the waters would sweep me away. Instead, I waded and splashed and fished from the edge. Still, I treasured those moments of freedom.

Even though the camps instilled a sense of maturity and independence, the rules of the community still applied at the camps. We learned that we were not entirely grown. Whenever we played too long and were late in returning the cattle, the elders would proffer a collective beating. As I was learning and often made mistakes, blisters and bruises became the norm for me. They were transition marks, meant to guide me into a herder's life. I didn't report these assaults to my father, as he would have dealt with my assaulters. I didn't wish to create further animosity with those who dealt my beatings. I instead acted as though I didn't care, and my resolve slowly earned me a grudging respect that soon dissolved into camaraderie. The cattle camp served to teach us how to herd and tend cattle, but it also functioned to instill the importance of the community. As the livelihood of our village depended on cows, we were taught to take our jobs seriously. We had to learn the time for work and the time for play.

In the evenings, after we did a headcount of the cattle and had them safely tethered, we enjoyed the freedom from a hard day's work. We played Adou and Alueeth, just as we did in the village, and while my milking skills were wanting, my ability to hit the ball in Adou earned me the approval of my peers. Wrestling matches were also periodically held amongst the elder boys and adults as entertainment. Sometimes, there would be wrestling matches between the champions of different camps, and the winner would receive the esteem of his audience. I was too young to wrestle, but I enjoyed cheering for the older youth in my camp.

After the evening games, we told riddles and stories before retiring for the night. We shared our favorite tales from our homes and often learned new stories from the youths of other villages. Later, we would attempt to retell these new tales as our own. Just like at home, storytelling was my favorite time of the day. I enjoyed the fabric of the words and how they wove in and out to pull me in as both participant and observer.

While we enjoyed the respite of games and stories, there was never complete freedom; raids were always an imminent threat, so we had to be continuously vigilant. Intermittently, the most feared of the raiders, called the Murle, the dreaded outlaws who killed adults, kidnapped children, and stole cows, attacked us. For protection against this constant danger, the older youth at camp served as guards for our community, defending the camp from these enemies, but if the enemy was too powerful, the youth beat a drum or burned a bush to alert the surrounding areas to join the fight. While I had experienced the Murle raids on the village, being in the cattle camp only a few short months, I only heard tales of these camp raids. I myself never had to fight or witness any form of raid until the fateful year of 1987.

In 1987, the government soldiers of Khartoum returned to our community. The Sudanese government knew that the SPLM/A had been recruiting soldiers from the Dinka villages and that many of the SPLM/A leaders were from the Dinka Bor community. The government wished to send a message, clear and final, to the villages. The attacks served as an act of pure revenge to the leaders of this rebel movement and as a warning to the men who considered joining the SPLM/A. With direct orders from the Khartoum government to annihilate the villages, the Arab soldiers aimed to destroy. They ruthlessly and methodically carried out the mission without questions.

In the dark of the night, the government soldiers attacked our cattle camp. The thunder of bombs and screams jolted me awake. Thinking it was a cattle raid by the Murle, my cousin and I ran from our hut and stepped into a world of flame from which there was no going back. There were people running in every direction, screaming in terror as Arab soldiers attacked and burned our cattle camp. Gunfire, sharp and unremitting, cascaded down upon us like rain. I froze beneath these scalding showers, horrified by the scene that unfolded before me. I watched aghast as those who were caught were butchered with knife, machetes, or bullets. The sound of the screams and of blade on bone pierced my own soul. I could only watch this carnage helplessly through eyes that burned with tears and smoke. Every fiber of my being screamed and screamed and screamed the silent scream of horror. Directionless, I ran, around the bodies of people and cattle that were scattered over the weeping earth.

I witnessed these Arab soldiers round up those they did not slaughter into groups. I later learned these prisoners were taken as captives to Khartoum. There was no method to who lived, who died; life, death was purely random. People ran and people fell. I fled this senseless devastation as they massacred innocent men, women, and children without reservation. Humanity had gone. It disappeared into the billows of smoke that rose from the murder of my people and my land. I have no words for the cries of raped and tortured women and children that will remain forever with me. With my mind, heart, and lungs choked with the screams and smoke, I ran, desperately and frantically, away from the terror.

Panic-stricken, I raced towards the village, seeking the refuge and protection of my family. As I had been taught, I fled with a group of boys from my camp. We sprinted through the fields and down the path towards my village and away from the madness. With the sounds of bombs and gunfire that grew louder as we drew nearer to our homes, our steps began to falter. No direction felt safe. This fear increased as we saw the spirals of smoke twisting like a snake into the sky. Our village was consumed in flame. Instead of shelter, I was welcomed by a wall of smoke and flames and wailing. I watched helplessly from a distance as my village went up in one huge conflagration. The sounds of gunfire, screams, and lamentations rose into the darkness of the night; a sound I will always equate with the cry of war.

The cloud of war had descended upon my village, one of the first communities to witness the destruction of this second Civil War. My village was destroyed, and thousands of villagers were forced to flee. With my family gone, I felt abandoned and afraid. As I watched the fires raging in the distance, at my home that no longer existed, I grew heavy with a sense of dread. Confounded with the ruins of my village, I quickly changed course and ran wildly and blindly, seeking the cover and safety of the jungle.

Chapter Two: Journey to the Unknown

Because many villages and cattle camps were destroyed by the raging inferno wrought upon them by hard and indiscriminate war, people scattered haphazardly in an attempt to escape the enemy's assault and rapidly spreading fire. Finding my way in the dark, I ran blindly, unable to stop to breathe and think. The words "Flee, flee, flee" drummed repetitively in my mind, keeping time to the beat of my pounding heart and desperate, racing footsteps. As I forced my way, I felt the surge of other bodies around me. Unable to discern if they were fellow escapees or enemy, I ran harder and faster.

When I fled far enough from the massacre, I halted, eyes burning and heart racing, and found myself in a crowd of young children and young adults, ages six through probably twelve, and a handful of older men. The eleven-to twelve-year-old boys, considered young adults, were some of the youth who were part of our cattle camp. We assembled on the spot, gasping and wheezing in shock, disbelief and exhaustion, with no way of determining if others survived or took other routes.

Among this drove of survivors, I could not locate anyone else from my part of the cattle camp. I searched frantically for my cousin who was with me at the camp during the attack, unable to find him. "Reech, Reech," I called in desperation. My watery eyes attempted to penetrate through the sea of people, but there was no answer, no familiar face. For the first time in my young life, I let loose a long piercing cry, born of raw rage, pain, and despair, that echoed from the core of my being and through the blackened forest. The other children suddenly cried out in a similar anguish. The echo of our cries multiplied, bouncing back and forth between our bodies, the forest, and the darkened night; the cry of war.

The attack had been well orchestrated, the surrounding villages destroyed. I stood among a countless throng of strangers from other villages. Since almost everybody that survived the fire and the massacre of the villages and cattle camps found different escape routes, the majority of our crowd had no relative or known adult. Although I rarely had witnessed adults cry, the few elders with us mumbled words of despondency and vulnerability as their eyes leaked soundless tears. Seeing these men, these pillars, crumble and mourn pierced my heart. The reality of our situation settled upon me like a dreadful weight.

I heard an elder's voice penetrate the cloud of disbelief surrounding us. "This is no time to grieve," he urged gently in an attempt to get us to move forward.

I turned around in a slow circle, seeking to get a bearing on my surroundings through the smoke-choked night. "Which way is forward? Where are we going?" I whispered in a stifled voice as I waited for a more definite direction.

Only the elder nearest to me heard my voice, and he offered words of consolation and hope: "Just keep going; our gods are our guides." The elders did not know our routes for certain; they only knew of the rumors of the SPLM/A leaders who defected to Ethiopia. Without any other option, they chose to try to lead us on this route.

Panic enveloped me once more. "I want to go home. I want my *Mama!*" I screamed. My cry didn't mean preference for one parent over another. To me, as a child, *Baba* was protection and strength; *Mama* was comfort and home, and home included my father. I wanted home; the safety, the comfort, the known, all that had been obliterated in but one moment of monstrous violence.

Other children picked up my cry, and together we keened, "I want to go home. I want to go home. I want my

Mama," into the indifferent night.

One of the elders sought to calm us and explained that we must flee to safety before we could head home. His words were a balm to us, but we still wanted our parents and home. I still harbored the hope that our families would find us once it was safe, just as they did during the raids when I was small. Part of me wanted to race towards the village and find my mother, yet the fear of meeting the same fate that befell my friends and neighbors, their bodies which had piled in twisted heaps before me, overruled my young conscience. I didn't want to be captured, and I didn't want to die. I had no choice but to trust in him, so I gathered my courage and prepared to follow him. As I fled away from my home with the rest of the group, my heart itself felt as though it were being scorched by the fires. My chest burned with tears, anger, and loss as I left my home for the unknown.

The elders endeavored to lead the way to safety, but none of them knew which direction to go, so we moved forward blindly, like the herds of animals we tended, but we had no shepherd, and we had no route. Eventually, rebel soldiers rescued us, and we began our endless trek towards Ethiopia. At the age of eight, I could not match the pace of the young and older men. As I lagged behind, my energy spent, I could hear my mother's warning: "The lion picks off the animal that strays from its herd." Not wanting to die, I pushed myself to keep up with the group, two steps to their one.

We pressed toward our destination, exhausted, thirsty, and starving; there was no food or water. We had to improvise, eating the scarce wild fruit and leaves as we could find them for breakfast, lunch, and dinner. Many of us perished from dehydration, starvation, or exertion. Some lost the will to keep going. I, too, languished in body and spirit, but I believed that if I kept going, I would see my family again.

As we were forced to flee in the night, we ran with what we wore on our backs. We had no provisions. Our clothing quickly became threadbare, so I, like many of my fellow refugees, walked barefoot and naked, exposed to the harsh elements, alternating between arid, unforgiving desert and relentless, saturating jungle rain. I ached - mind, body, and spirit.

As we journeyed through the desert, we traveled between fire and ice. During the day, we were baked from above and below, by sky and earth. The searing sun blazed ceaselessly down upon our parched, fatigued bodies and turned the sand into an oven that blistered and seared our weary feet. In the nights, the heat escaped with the sun, and we froze, but after the unrelenting thirst and burning, I found some respite in these frigid nights that shivered and rattled my bones. In the torrid days, the pain of the heat erased all thought except for the struggle to keep going. It was in the silence of these cold, endless nights that I was able to feel, to mourn the loss of my family. I yearned for the comforts of my home, the warmth of a shirt, of a blanket - of my mother. In my longing, I felt closer to her somehow.

Typically, though, we walked at night, as the elders believed the night offered a cover from our enemies, and in the daytime, we were forced to walk faster; there wasn't time for rest. Our bodies soon slackened from thirst. We could not go on. I, along with many other boys, sunk to the ground, too weakened to continue. I watched in fascinated horror as some of the elders urinated into their hands and then drank this urine to sustain themselves. As is typical of dreadful deeds, they hold a certain magnetism. I could only stare. I recoiled when elders urged us to do the same. "No way," I said. "There's no way I'm going to drink pee." I cringed with disgust. One of the elders sternly responded,

"If you do not do what it takes to survive, you will die." This statement humbled me. As I did not want to die, I urinated into my hands. At first, the bitter acridness made me gag, but my thirst overpowered my apprehension, and I shamelessly gulped this repellent liquid.

After about ten endless days and nights in the desert, we made it to the semi-desert, where there stood an occasional leafless tree. When we would see the rare and beautiful bones of a tree standing before us, we rushed to steal a few minutes reprieve in the shadow of its skeleton. The elders tolerated these for moments of respite, as their bodies and spirits had also been pressed harshly. We moved like this through the desert - walking and stopping, our skeleton bodies huddled beneath a skeleton tree.

Once we made it to the jungle, we raised our faces to the canopy of trees overhead in communal exaltation. The shade, the liberation from a punishing sun, felt blessed in its relief. However, the rains soon came in a ceaseless flood of cold drizzle that turned both the grounds and us into sodden mush. At the first appearance of water, I, like those about me, began to gulp from this benevolent fount, desperately attempting to quell the fires of dehydration. However, the elders advised us to slow down. For many, thirst overpowered the warning. I lay flat upon my back on the damp ground, as my stomach contracted in painful spasms; I was unable to move, and from the groans about me, I was not alone in my agony. Some did not survive.

After the painful paroxysms subsided, we began our slow trudge through the infinite mud and water. The chilled damp seeped into my skin as my teeth chattered from the cold. I gazed at my fellow travelers, and they, like me, hugged their midsections, their eyes huge and drowned in the middle of their strained faces. With our skin chilled and shriveled and our bodies hunched in an effort to retain warmth, we looked like a group of miniature, wrinkled old men rather than children.

As we struggled onward, we faced yet another threat, imminent and dangerous, inhabitants of the jungle - lions, tigers, hyenas, wolves, and they took advantage of our weakness. Our desiccated forms served as a period of feasting for them. These jungle beasts preferred to pick off the stragglers; not unlike humans, they fear groups and prefer to target the weak. Here, in this dire situation, our lessons from cattle camp carried over. We huddled as a group in the center of the road and walked as one. As I heard the guttural growls of the lions and the pained, panicked screams of those who could no longer keep up, I shuddered from a heady combination of guilt and fear and drew myself even closer to the center of the group. Panting, cold, exhausted, I knew I could not fall behind.

Our journey continued, alternating between these harsh terrains of dry and wet, and my fatigue soon became palpable, my spirit whittled down by my weakened and hungered body. I no longer possessed the strength or the will left to live. I began to long for death. Like a desert mirage that beckons the weary traveler toward waters he or she will never reach, death appeared as a welcome end to my loss, my hunger, my weariness. At that moment of complete physical and spiritual exhaustion, I felt as though I had reached my end; yet, I realize now that a deeper and stronger part of me longed to live, as every night, while I yearned for death, images of the cattle camp, my family's compound, my parents, and my siblings filled me with hope, and I clung desperately to this hope instead of to the illusion of death.

As we continued our journey, to boost the spirits of all who walked, the elders led us in song. The singing comforted me like my mother's lullabies, and I sang with all of my might. The elders led us in a song that we sang during our cattle camp days, and this song became my source of strength and inspiration for life. We sang in unison, and when no one else was singing, I sang by myself:

Muk yï piɔu rïny lɔ wɛɛr wɛɛr roor.

Jeny ce yic diil wɛɛi ë root acïn tɔŋ ye thɔ̈ɔ̈r ke cinic ka gëi ëke

Ɣɛndɛ! Cɔkku röth ril, wɔ berë ke cak pinyda awel rot

Jeny ë Dïtoor athär yic nyic Nhialic. Na pïr raan ku rum pinyde, ke bï ŋuëën ŋö.

Cakkë thäär abï naŋ adhëŋ töŋ döŋ, Kɔth de baai, Thudän panda

Acuk bï com në kë peei, Aaye wɔ nyïn wɔ jeny mɛn thäär

Duye diɛɛr në thou. Tariir ë tɔŋ ë Thudän Junub, abï mɛnh kënë dhiëëth nyic aköldë

Yic näk wɔ yen kë, awai tiɔmda, Tiɔm cït awaai.

wɔ ce abaköök cam pan lei. Wɔ ka ya döy ke baai

Tiɔm cï rim kuɔ dhiɔ̈m, abï tɔ̈ɔ̈kda boot. Yic abï tuɔl, nɔŋ tiɔm ku wun

Baai acït nyin wɔ, thër ku baai ne ŋeeeny lɔcäp.

The song translates,

"Be hopeful, scattered generation. You the army, which has strengthened itself, encourage yourself. There is no war without surprises. Yes, let's be strong. We are being recreated. Our land is going through changes. The Sudan People's Liberation Army of Dr. John Garang is fighting for our truth known to God. A person without land is lifeless. Let's fight. There will be a survivor, a seed of the nation. Our Sudan will never be sown with different seeds, but us. So don't fear death. The liberation of South Sudan will be known to unborn generations because we are sacrificing lives for our sweet land. We are not immigrants. We are the natives of this home, a land which has drained our blood, but it will fill our wounds. The truth will emerge because every land knows its owner. Our land looks like us. Let's fight with courage. Our nation is going backward, so let's invoke God to come down. God, who created human beings, and designated territories, mark the boundaries, so that we are free forever."

This song, with our raised voices, felt like water to my parched soul. The motivational lyrics gave me a reason to keep going, to fight - to live. Here we were, exhausted beyond the realm of human limits, yet we stood, withered and depleted - and singing. With our voices strong and determined, I chose life. I believe, in this moment, we all chose life.

Sensing this shift in spirit, the elders, although they themselves were weary, offered us words of encouragement and hope. Their voices continually sounded, "You're a Dinka, and the gods of the Dinka are with you; be strong and do not give up." As I listened to these simple, hope-filled words, I felt strength gathering within me. I felt spiritually empowered. When I heard these words spoken by the prayerful, weak voices of our elders, I realized that we were not just running for our lives; we were running for the survival of our society. With our escape, we were ensuring the continuation of our people. We were the hope of our future.

After walking for more than forty-five days, we came, starving and exhausted, to a great river, that stood between us and a refugee camp in Ethiopia. On the other side of the shore, we stared in surprised disbelief as a group of South Sudanese excitedly jumped up and down, waving their arms and calling to us that we had reached the end of our journey. We were told that we had reached Pinyudo, so, at the time, that is what we called this great river; we later learned that the river was the Tana River, which borders southwestern

Ethiopia. We did not have a plan when we fled our village. We did not know where we were going. We merely walked and walked with the hope of finding a safe and peaceful haven. And now, now that we were finally there, so close to our destination, we were taunted by a body of water over which we could only shout from shore to shore.

The sheer immensity of this river and its rushing waves was unlike anything I had previously encountered. Like the roar of a lion, it commanded respect, and I stood before it with a mixture of awe, fear, and discouragement. Had we perhaps encountered these waters on a peaceful journey, I would have watched in wonder as the waves methodically pounded the banks of the river with speed and precision. Instead, I stood disheartened before its shore. This great river prevailed as the only obstacle between us and the conclusion of our perilous journey. I stared out over the boundless, surging waters, not knowing how I could possibly amass the energy to make it to the other side. I suddenly felt incomprehensibly small.

As I approached the riverbank, I spotted sunbathing creatures that rolled and crawled on the sand, stretching wide jaws of knife-like teeth that shone as ominously as bared bone. We halted and gazed in horror as these deadly beasts plunged into the river and disappeared. Although they vanished from sight, we sensed their vigilant, watchful eyes upon us from beneath the seemingly smooth mirror of water. These furtive brutes were the crocodiles of the Tana River.

As the elders tried to plan how to cross these deceptive waters, many children jumped into the river to swim, the temptation of the cool, mirrored waters too much to resist after such an arduous journey. I stood helplessly, silent screams choked in my throat, as I witnessed the crocodiles devour the majority of those who had leapt innocently into the waters, as others succumbed to the treacherously fatal waves. Upon witnessing our hardship, the Anyuak, the native Ethiopians who live along the riverbank, offered to ferry us to the other side in their handmade, wooden boats. The first boat capsized in the river's dark, misleading waters and killed all thirty people on board. The process was immediately halted. We spent a night on the cold sand, the river a hurdle between us and the camps on the other side. Even in my exhaustion, I could not rest. I dreaded the passage and worked to steel myself to make this exigent journey.

At first light, the refugees on the other shore reappeared, and the elders and native Ethiopians sought once more to cross to Ethiopia's Pinyudo refugee camp. I stood paralyzed with horror, images of my comrades lost to this river fresh in my mind, as the elders gently urged me down to its mammoth waters. I felt nauseated from fear. If my boat capsized, I would be surely lost. I did not know how to swim. I climbed with hesitant and trembling limbs onto the crude, rudimentary boat and knelt, placing my palms flat upon the wood as though the solidity beneath my hands would protect me from the heaving world around me. The other boys, the terror in their eyes matching my own, boarded the boat and mirrored my prayerful pose, while the boys who knew how to swim jumped in unison into the waters by the boats to swim alongside our wooden rafts. They believed the sound and wave of their great splash would deter the unseen crocodiles from preying on them.

Clinging to anything that grounded my fear; the rough of the wood and the splash of bodies ,the Ethiopians began our slow transport across the river. The boat rocked precariously across the moving waters as we climbed and plummeted the swell of the waves, the waters dousing us in warning. My heart throbbed uncontrollably as the cold, metallic taste of fear curdled sour in my mouth.

After what seemed like an eternity, we reached the shore. The other refugees gave us a hand to help us out of the boats and water and talked fervently to us. I learned they had been there for about a month. I waded shakily from the boat to the riverbank, my body and limbs still quaking uncontrollably with the precariousness of the crossing, as well as from a new sense of elation. We made it. We had reached our destination. I was overjoyed. Attempting to halt the rocking motion of my body and grateful for the solidity of the cool, hard, ground beneath my feet, I walked unsteadily to join the group gathered on the bank. Without pause, the Pinyudo refugees began to lead us the short distance to Pinyudo. We commenced on the final stretch of our journey. In my exhaustion, I honestly couldn't believe I survived the journey, that I made it to the camp, but as one of my colleagues once put it, "We followed the bones." The bones of those who passed before us, of those who succumbed to dehydration, exhaustion, or fell prey to animal attacks, marked our path to Ethiopia. Death had led us to safety.

Finally in Pinyudo, we found ourselves among an immeasurable sea of skeletal boys. I had never seen so many people. I took in the camp, which consisted of nothing but a cluster of crude makeshift shelters constructed of grass and trees by the refugees there. As we were bade welcome, I listened to the tales of how the people there went for days without eating. As I looked at the lack of solid homes, stared into the hollowed eyes of these starved souls, heard their tales of hunger, I became overwhelmed with a sense of disheartenment; the journey, the suffering seemed futile. We had walked for miles seeking safety and shelter only to suffer further. At home, I had my hut, my family. Here, there was nothing. I slowly took in this inhospitable and unfamiliar wasteland and wondered if I would survive.

Over the next couple of days, we endeavored to locate our friends and relatives among the multitude of people. I anxiously searched for Reech, fearing he was dead, yet the crowd was too great to penetrate. I slowly sunk to my knees, defeated and alone, amid this massive band of survivors of nearly thirty-thousand parentless boys.

Chapter Three: A New Beginning

Shocked and disheartened by the desolate scene before me, I picked myself up from the dusty earth and began to wander aimlessly, searching in vain for a familiar face. My hopes, at this point, had plummeted. The lack of family, homes, and food weighed heavily upon my young mind. After about three days of inquiring about Reech and my family, a group of Aboudit found me wandering, dazed and hungry about the camp and invited me to join them. I choked back tears of relief and gladly accepted their invitation. I followed my fellow Aboudit community members to their area in the camp. As many of the tribes of South Sudan did not get along, the refugees of the camp segregated themselves into communities. Upon arriving to the Aboudit's area, my cousin Reech, who I became separated from during the Arab attack on our village, rushed tearfully out to greet me. My heart surged with joy to find him alive, yet I was shocked by his emaciated appearance. His face betrayed the same astonishment at my appearance. The journey had taken its toll on both of us. When I inquired as to the whereabouts of my family, Reech just clasped my hands and shook his head sadly. He had no news of my family or his own.

While I felt extreme gratitude in being reunited with my cousin and companion, I expected to find my family, to again have the comforts of love, food, and protection. Instead, I faced this desolate, hungry camp parentless. My family dominated my mind, which increased my sense of anxiety and loneliness. I felt as though my horrific journey had been in vain. I remained separated from my family, a sorrowful position that earned me a new title, "Lost Boy of Sudan," a title which, at the time, mirrored the emptiness that I felt. Still, I clung to the belief that it would be only days before I would reunite with my family. Unfortunately, days became weeks, weeks became months, and months became years.

The Pinyudo refugee camp stood in the midst of a dry, desiccated land, a land barren and unforgiving. The natives were dealing with famine, and we arrived, already starved from our passage, to their land during this impossible time. We found no relief from our arduous journey, from our pain, from the searing hunger that tyrannically ruled our lives. With scarcely any fertile land for farming, most of the Anyuak, the native Ethiopians of the area, were also starving, so we had great difficulty finding something to eat. We were forced to scavenge for any sustenance we could find. I awoke in the morning to spend all day searching for food with my fellow refugees. We meticulously scoured the parched soil in the vain hope of finding remnants of food from earlier harvests. Sometimes we found bits of fallen grain and corn. With little on the ground, we soon extended our search to the garbage dumps in the nearby area of Pinyudo where the shops were located. No matter how long we searched, we never found enough to eat. The elders, when they succeeded in finding food, shared the little they found and ended up starving themselves.

Occasionally, the sympathetic Anyuak, starving themselves, brought us small rations of maize and beans. The visits were infrequent, and there was usually only one cup of maize or bean grain for ten people, but this great gift from a poor people astounded me; they had so little, yet they still gave to us, strangers to them - a poignant, simple truth that both touched and consoled me. While this small amount of food did little to quell our hunger, this gift, immense in a time of starvation, made the difference between life and death. Unfortunately, this generous gift of grain was not worth cooking, but it was all there was at the time - for them and us. While we carefully poured the hard, dry kernels into the fire to roast, as cautious as we were with this precious food source, some of it always slipped into the ashes, like sand through a sieve.

As we could hardly subsist on the scarce cups of maize or grain, we continued to scavenge and gathered the scarce leaves and wild fruits in a desperate attempt to sate our starving stomachs. We quickly learned that not all of the fruits and leaves were edible. Some people ate poisonous leaves or fruits and died, writhing in agony. In this purgatory, I could not tell which was worse, a quick, painful death by poison or a slow, drawn out death by starvation. Yet I was not ready for death. My survival instincts took over, and I ate whatever I could find. Too soon, as Pinyudo stood in the middle of a semi-desert and there were few trees, we ran out of this food source as well.

Over the course of only two months, I, along with everybody else in the camp, became a walking skeleton, a mere shadow of my old self. Deprived of food, medical attention, and clean water, I witnessed many people die of hunger and disease, a direct result of the unsanitary atmosphere of the refuge to which we had escaped. The absence of sanitation due to overcrowding and a lack of medical resources led to unfortunate and uncontrolled outbreaks of dysentery and cholera. And, in the middle of this desolation, hunger loomed ominously - none were spared.

Hovering darkly over me, hunger ruled me, twisting his slow, torturous blade. From the moment I woke up to the moment I went to bed, hunger dominated my desiccated existence. It was a twenty-four/seven ravenous hunger, a hunger that hollowed out my already emaciated form, and I soon became too weak to leave my sad, make-shift shelter. I just stared into space, hoping for a miracle, for some sort of divine intervention to end my suffering. Feeling forgotten and abandoned, I felt myself begin to slip away.

In these pained moments of near starvation, I visualized nothing but food and my short idyllic life before I left my village. I conjured up images of my parents at home, my father farming in the compound and my mother helping him to plant seeds. Then I'd see my mother in the kitchen preparing plenty of food. Sweet, intoxicating aromas wafted about me as she prepared her peanut paste and pumpkin porridge. She gathered everybody together to eat. I sat by the bowls of food with my father and brothers, but when I went to take a bite of her food, I lifted empty air to my mouth and was jerked back to the reality of torturous, cramping hunger. Tears flew to my eyes.

As starvation consumed me, my cousin Reech fell terribly ill and was admitted to the clinic that lacked doctors, nurses, and medicine. Without proper medical supplies, this clinic merely served as a place where people went to die. It functioned to quarantine the sick in the hopes of halting the spread of infection, and its slim and untrained staff attempted to keep the ill comfortable. Drained of power and energy and heedless of becoming infected myself, I went to stay with Reech, filled with hope that he would get well. I refused to become discouraged. We had come so far together, and I knew that, without parents, the responsibility of Reech's well-being was mine. I sat and started to pray for him, but his illness would not release its cruel clasp. He suffered from what seemed to be diarrhea, and, in time, I learned that he had fallen prey to the same sickness as the other camp victims - cholera. The sight of Reech, already skeletal, growing even more and more lean by the second tore at the fabric of my soul. I felt helpless. I turned to the elders for help, but they were busy with a more immediate task - disposing of the bodies of the children, men, and women who had fallen victim to the calamity.

Full of desperation, I hung on to my cousin and continued to pray for his recovery. I will never forget the moment when my cousin looked at me through vacant eyes and whispered, "Chol, I feel weak," as a single tear slid down his dry, papery cheek.

"No, Reech," I said, as I squeezed his limp child's hand in my own, holding onto it as though it were a lifeline. I willed strength into him. "Reech, you are going to be fine," I assured him, even as he started to breathe more and more slowly. I sobbed and clung to the hope that he would recover. I cried myself to sleep at Reech's bedside, and when I awoke, he lay on his bed, peaceful and still. I thought that he, too, had fallen asleep.

As I continued to sit in watch at his bed, an elder came along and gently touched my shoulder. "I am so sorry, my son," he had said. "Your cousin is gone." Reech, my cousin, my comrade, my best friend, became but one of the many dead refugees buried unmarked in a mass grave.

As I buried my cousin, I awakened to the agonizing truth that he was gone. I sobbed, wracked with tears of sorrow, and attempted to throw myself into his grave. My distant relatives and friends carried me away from his grave and comforted me. With my cousin gone, I was forced to face the harshness of a refugee life with no immediate relative. I now had to live with the cruel combination of hunger and grief.

After I lost my cousin, I had no choice but to mix with strangers I didn't know. Reech's death left an ache, a hole inside of me, and I felt pervasively alone. I knew nothing of my life other than it became a torturous, day-to-day survival. By day, I wandered listlessly beneath the face of the grilling sun scavenging for scraps of food. Sometimes, in the early hours of night, parched and weary, I tried to play with boys my age like I used to with my siblings before my mother brought food, but exhaustion and hunger were too powerful. The exertion sent me into a heap on the dusty ground, where I would sleep as though someone was going to come and wake me for dinner. No one ever came. In their own hunger, the boys, my only friends, did not want to share their food with one more mouth. I awoke countless times in the middle of the night, with dust-clogged mouth and nostrils, as the ravenous blade of hunger continued to carve out my already empty stomach. I could never go back to sleep. Sometimes I dragged myself back to my shelter, while most often I lay there, too weak to move, a still and starving body upon the earth. This unending torment established itself as the routine of my life.

Soon, I succumbed to illness and lost consciousness of my surroundings. This time, there was mercy. One elder boy, Peter Anyieth Mayen, a boy I knew only in passing, served as my savior, my good Samaritan. I awoke in a rudimentary shelter, Peter by my side. He spoke a few words to me before I again passed out, weakened by starvation and illness.

After my strength began to return, Peter recounted my illness to me in detail. He had found me curled in the dust outside, my breathing barely detectable. The leaders wished to place me in the clinic, where my cousin Reech spent his last hours. Peter, however, appealed passionately to the leaders; he begged them not to take me to the crowded and dirty clinic where, he believed, I would surely die.

Reluctantly, as they did not want my illness to spread through the camp, the leaders submitted to Peter's plea, and Peter carried me to his makeshift shelter where, in keeping with the traditional native medicine, he treated me with leaves. Thankfully, God responded kindly. Peter assured me,

"You survived because God refused to give up on your life." To this day, I believe that God spared my life, that I survived for a reason, and to this day, I only pray to be worthy of the life I have been granted.

Peter, this stranger, in his gentle kindness, understood that I was alone, one small boy clinging to a rudimentary existence in this unforgiving environment. Although the living space in his hut, a rude rectangular structure of wood and mud and grass, was already cramped with ten to fifteen other boys, Peter, who belonged to a different subgroup of Dinka Bor than me, took me into his home and became my friend and savior when I needed one the most. With someone to care for me, life no longer felt like an endless battle.

After two months of suffering in the refugee camp, the Ethiopian government was able to attract the attention of humanitarian organizations and prevailed upon them to help us. The first two organizations to offer assistance were the United Nations Children's Fund (UNICEF) and the United Nations High Commissioner for Refugees (UNHCR). With the arrival of their food-laden trucks, everything changed. For the first time in months, we had plenty to eat and a variety of foods from which to choose. Beans, lentils, flour, oil, and fruits were slowly introduced to us until we were no longer hungry. With the locals, we swapped some of the grain for much needed meat. We had so much food that we shared some of the extras with the hungry Ethiopians who had helped us in our time of need.

No longer starving, we began to grow settled in the refugee camp. Then the UNHCR announced their plan to regroup us. While we originally had formed our own kinship based groups, the UNHCR regrouped us to ensure that people from different families and clans were put together. In Sudan, we were used to living together in big families and small communities made up of clans. The purpose of this new grouping was to create both a clan and a community from the diverse population in the refugee camp. Thus, relationships not based on kinship were formed. We began to learn about each other and form bonds of kinship that transcended our tribal boundaries.

At first it was difficult to be intimate with strangers, especially those we considered enemies in the past. After all, South Sudanese are not homogeneous. They fought each other and some raided other villages for their cattle. At first, living among strangers, rivals, and those we were raised to view as enemies was uncomfortable, but we soon adjusted and began to work together in a unified group - our daily existence, as well as our joy, depended upon our collaboration.

In 1988, not long after this regrouping, the UNHCR announced their plan to open schools for us. This new concept "school" was foreign to me. I felt both frightened and curious. The UN had tried to hire Ethiopian teachers but couldn't afford their salaries, not to mention the teacher-student ratio was overwhelming, so they brought in SPLM teachers to educate us. For the first time in my life, I began going to school.

We started classes under the tree but were later forced to build our own schools with mud and grass. A blackboard was built onto the wall for the teachers to use for instruction and for us to practice our lessons. However, there were not enough textbooks or exercise books. We shared a textbook, and one exercise book was cut into three pieces for three students to share for homework and exams. Using fingers on sand or dirt, we learned to write our alphabet and numbers on the ground. At times, teachers pressed our fingers onto the ground for proper calligraphy. The force and physicality of these teachers' frustrations frightened me.

I, like my fellow Lost Boys, started in first grade, but it was not easy because education had never been a part of my culture. School was not a joy at all to me. I, like my friends, didn't want to go because its significance lay far beyond my imagination. However, taking the role of our parents, the UN devised a plan. For the next six months, the UN enticed us to school with clothes and biscuits; if we chose not to go to school, we went hungry for that day, and as we did not wish to starve, we went to school. Thus, with these powers of persuasion, the UN baited us into laying a foundation for our own future.

Soon after this clever trickery, our teachers made it mandatory to go to school, and punitive measures were put in place. Whoever chose not to go to school received lashes and extra chores. After the stinging whip, the truants were forced to collect firewood, poles, and grass for building. As we were unused to school, these punishments incited resentment rather than a love of learning.

Shortly after we began this punitive education, Dr. John Garang, the SPLM leader, visited our camp, and our teachers informed us that he wished to speak to us. Dr. Garang had become like a legend to me, to all of us. I first learned of him when my father told me he hid in our village, which made me view my village as special. I grew up singing songs about how he was leading South Sudan and my people to freedom. Hearing that this celebrated SPLM leader wished to speak with us, I felt overcome with feelings of awe, excitement, and, more powerfully, rage. I wanted justice, to make our attackers pay for destroying my home. Like all Dinka boys, I was a potential soldier born to defend my community, and I wanted to join the fight against our common enemy, as did my fellow classmates. So with hearts filled with vengeance, we gathered to hear Dr. Garang speak, anxious to be called upon to avenge and defend our land, homes, and family. To our surprise, Dr. Garang's vision was different.

In his speech, he asserted, "Wars are fought, but after winning, there is a need for development. We are fighting because our future is you. You, the youth, are the 'seeds of our nation.' We count on you to become doctors, engineers, politicians, diplomats, pilots, and leaders of all kinds for New Sudan." He continued, "For now, your responsibility is education."

Dr. Garang's speech, which reaffirmed that I am the future of my people, echoed the words of my father. Hearing these proclamations once more, and from this eminent leader, sparked something deep in the core of my being; a revolution flared within my spirit. My desire for revenge grew small beside these words that forever changed my life. I realized that I, as a living, breathing person, am a part of the true capital of my country, the hope for its future. I knew that I was a capital for my family and probably for my community; however, I never before thought of myself as a seed of a nation. At this moment, even though I didn't yet understand the impact education would have on my life, I chose to pursue education as my path. I wished to make a difference, to be one of the seeds that would bring positive change to my country. I could only stare as Dr. Garang departed.

Even though Dr. Garang returned to his base, the Sudan People's Liberation Movement's base in Bilpam, near the Sudan-Ethiopia border, his words, encouraging and hopeful, resonated within me. In fact, his words continue to impact me as I continue to strive in pursuit of education in order to make a difference for my country.

Because the UN was unable to hire teachers, Dr. Garang kept his promise, and, to my excitement, in a few days, we received more teachers from the SPLM/A. Most of the teachers were students, who dropped out of Sudan high schools and universities to join the SPLM/A for the liberation of the marginalized people. However, while their qualifications were limited, their arrival raised the level of the meager education we had been receiving.

In addition, the SPLM/A also sent a camp manager, who added a new level of organization within the refugee camp and our school. This camp manager organized a board of education within the refugee camp with the hopes of improving the education system. He coordinated with UN personnel on education and camp issues, appointed caregivers and head teachers, and set up a security administration within the camp. Life began to take on an order and a structure.

For four years, we went to school, a novelty for most of us who had never entered a classroom in our lives. We were divided into groups of about one hundred to one hundred and fifty and placed in different classes, each marked with a different number and letter of the alphabet. On the first day, we were told to remember our classroom letter and number, and each day, we were to return to our assigned classroom. I was assigned to Class 1A. Here, in these classes, a camaraderie formed as we grew comfortable with our classmates, and, as the class sizes were so large, we grew especially close with our benchmates.

At school, we were primarily taught from three books, provided by the UN; *The New Friends*, *Hallo Children*, and *Read With Us*. *The New Friends*, which contained many stories that stressed the importance of unity, taught us the value of friendship and the importance of interacting with one another in a friendly manner. It reinforced our appreciation of the broader relationships that extended beyond our tribes that were being established in living amongst each other. We were slowly losing our ethnocentric tribalistic sentiments that had been ingrained in us from birth as we learned the importance of being a part of something larger - a nation, a continent, humanity. *Hallo Children* taught us the value of childhood to society and how children develop and play. As we had always worked for our families and communities, the concept of childhood was strange to us. Fascinated by the children in this book, we attempted to imitate their games and learned new ways to play. The third book, *Read With Us*, a second grade text, promoted reading, writing, listening, and speaking skills. Each of these texts were chosen to foster friendship among the different tribes in the camp and to help us understand the importance of education.

In time, we realized that the NGOS deliberately unified us to prevent future wars and genocide. In forcing us to live amongst each other and attend school together, they were attempting to get us to see each other - and our world - beyond the narrow lenses of our tribes. They hoped that the relationships that we forged at the camp would prove lasting and that we would be positive examples of unity to the other Sudanese when we returned to our homes.

Soon after we settled into our new homes, schools, and friendships, Rev. Andrew Mayol Ajak, who was sent by Bishop Nathaniel Garang Anyieth, "The Lost Bishop," arrived to teach us about Christianity. Bishop Nathaniel Garang Anyieth had been ordained as the Bishop of Bor just before the attacks on the villages. He, like the other villagers, was forced to flee. A refugee himself, Bishop Anyieth dedicated his time traveling among the refugee camps in an attempt to introduce the Christian God to the refugees. As the majority of refugees were "Lost Boys," Bishop Anyieth earned the title "The Lost Bishop." As he couldn't be in all of the camp areas at once, he recruited other religious figures to help him spread his Christian message. Although missionary work reached Bor in 1905 through Archibald Shaw, a missioner stationed in Malek, South of Bor, I had never heard a name like Christ. I was raised in an animist community that believed in one supreme God - the creator - and many lesser, more immediate gods. On special occasions, people believed to possess special powers in my community personified our gods; they read the future and interpreted various problems. Each community also possessed well-known and powerful gods, represented by village totems, as well as small and less powerful gods for the subsections of their community.

Church and bible study, like school, were mandatory, so I arrived at the church, my stomach churning with a mixture of nervousness, curiosity, and confusion. I listened raptly as Rev. Andrew stood in the pulpit and preached about God and Jesus Christ. For the first time, I heard the Christian message, that there is only one God whose son is Jesus Christ who died on the cross for us. "Why did he die?" we asked. "He died to redeem us from our sins," he answered. He continued, "Although you do not know him, he was the one that guided you here to safety, and he will be the one to bring peace to our warring country and return you to Sudan."

The sermon made me feel very special and fortunate. However, I wondered about those who did not survive the journey to the refugee camp. "Have they sinned before God?" I asked myself. Rev. Andrew interrupted my thoughts by continuing with his message. "Faith is very important in order to be a Christian," he said. "If you believe in Christ, you will never die; you will go to heaven where there is no suffering and death." He then quoted John 3:16, "God loved the world so much that he gave his one and only son, so that whoever believes in him may not die, but have eternal life. God sent Jesus so that the old becomes new." These words touched me because I believed that what I went through - my suffering, my pain, and my survival - was a testimony of God's presence. I couldn't wait for the sermon to be over. I wanted to quickly convert to Christianity to get everlasting life.

The tradition of becoming a Christian is unique in South Sudan. People are required to pick a biblical name because they are believed to be holy. While I had many names to choose from, I had difficulty deciding between Abraham and Nathaniel. I liked the sound of these two names above all of the others. There were individuals with such names in my class, those whose families had converted when the missionaries came through the villages. As few people had converted, these names were strange to me, and during roll-call, I admired their soft, rolling sounds. I just wanted to know their meaning from the Pastor. The Pastor informed me that Abraham means "father of multitude" and Nathaniel "gift from God." I felt that the only reason I survived the perilous journey was because I was a gift from God, so I chose Nathaniel during baptism.

I immediately loved my Christian life, and I planned to one day return home and convert all of my family, and, if possible, my entire clan or community so that we could reunite in heaven when we die. With my new sense of purpose, I pursued my education and excelled at school. I soon completed fourth grade.

Despite the care we were receiving from the UNHCR, some of the refugees in the camp grew deeply depressed - they longed to be home with family and clan members; however, many of us also adjusted to the circumstance at the refugee camp. While I still longed for my family, I was very thankful for the care and education I was receiving through the UN, and my depression over the loss of my family began to lessen. Dr. John Garang's message of unity and optimism,

God's biblical promises, and my education had filled me with a new hope for a better future. Life in the refugee camp was growing beautiful because of one thing - learning.

These hopes, unfortunately, came to an abrupt end. The war had followed us, and in 1991, due to the Ethiopian civil war, we lost everything we had begun so desperately to rebuild. The Ethiopian rebels overthrew the Ethiopian president, Mengistu Haile Mariam, a friend of Dr. John Garang and the South Sudanese. Supported by the government in Khartoum, these insurgents toppled the Ethiopian government, and as they suspected the SPLM/A of supporting the deposed president, they disliked our presence.

Every day for weeks, refugees arrived in droves from the Itang, a South Sudanese refugee camp in western Ethiopia. They claimed to have been chased at gunpoint by rebels who just ousted the president. Our leadership did not heed their warnings. We continued with our daily lives; however, the atmosphere grew heavy with tension.

Shortly after these cautionary stories, soldiers from the SPLA arrived. I watched in alarm as the SPLA soldiers spoke with the camp manager. I couldn't hear what they were saying, but I could see his posture grow erect as his expression shifted from a mask of fear to one of determination as he quickly sought out our caretakers.

An unfamiliar caretaker approached my group. "You need to prepare to leave immediately. The enemy soldiers are on their way."

Trepidation seized my heart in its paralyzingly cold grasp. We had to leave Pinyudo, a place where I had just begun to find comfort. We were ordered to leave behind our heavy belongings; we needed to move fast.

Our camp turned into a flurry of movement as we prepared to flee. As we readied for our hasty departure, the Ethiopian rebel soldiers, under the leadership of Meles Zenawi, charged into the camp. I fled with the other Lost Boys at gunpoint. Images of these Ethiopian rebels blurred with my memories of Sudanese Arabs who had attacked my village, a picture forever burned into my mind. I had but one thought: "Not again." Once more, I ran for my survival.

Chapter Four: Out of Ethiopia

I will never forget the first day of our journey. While Pinyudo was far from a home, it had been a sanctuary for nearly four years, and I was terrified to leave once more for the unknown. My first journey was tinged with an intangible horror my young mind could not grasp; it was a flight from the unreal. This second journey, now that I fully grasped that hatred and inhumanity existed, felt all too real. War has the ability to do that, to shatter illusion. I didn't want the limbo of a nomadic life, of having no place, again. I felt hunted. Our caretakers and teachers instructed us to stay in groups and urged everyone not to rest until we were safe. We walked quickly in our groups with the knowledge that we were being pursued.

I will never forget the heat of the day, blistering and constant, yet the instinct of survival drove me and the other boys to continue. After hours of walking in the torrid heat, as my strength wavered and many of the boys around me began to fall, it started to rain. I tilted my face to the sky and spread my arms wide in welcome. I shared this moment of relief with the other boys, who likewise looked skyward. We looked a sight - a bunch of skinny homeless boys standing smiling in the rain. Everything - clothes, bags, food, and body - grew saturated. The way became soggy and muddy, but the liberating coolness brought comfort to our journey. For the rest of the day, we no longer felt the heat.

In the evening, a day and a half later, we arrived in Gilo One. Gilo, divided by the Gilo River, lies partly in Ethiopia, Gilo One, and partly in Sudan, Gilo Two. For all of our safety, we needed to make it out of Ethiopian territory and into Sudan. When we finally arrived at the Gilo, this divisor between life or death, rather than welcoming us with safety, raged against the shores. The river was flooded. In the darkness, the danger of drowning and crocodiles was too great. We were faced with probable death by water or possible death by fire, and to our growing anxiety, we were forced to spend a night in Gilo One.

As I stood once more before a river that served as a blockade to safety, I found it incredible that one river could serve such a divide - between war and safety, life and death. The ridiculousness of these human-drawn lines still does not fail to astonish me, how the mere fault of birth makes one friend or foe. The adults stood guard to ensure the safety of our group, yet with the all-too-recent memories of our attack and with the knowledge we were still being pursued, I slept a fitful sleep.

The following day, Salva Kiir Mayardit, second in command of the SPLM, now the current president of South Sudan, arrived with a platoon to inform us that the Ethiopian rebels had taken over Pinyudo refugee camp. "You need to move. Now!" he ordered. As we were still in Ethiopian territory and the rebels were in swift pursuit, he ordered everybody to cross to Gilo 2 at once. The fear this news brought sparked a new sense of urgency in all of us. I feared another confrontation with the North Sudanese soldiers and was ready to leave Ethiopia as soon as possible. Adding to my increasing anxiety, I saw a mirror of this apprehension on the other Lost Boys' faces. Yet, even through this fear, I felt a spark of hope. While I knew we would not be traveling close to South Sudan, I would be closer to my family than I had been in four years. I longed to go home.

I quickly gathered with the other boys on the banks of an angry Gilo. I could only stare and wait. The local inhabitants soon arrived with wooden boats. The boats loaded the youngest of the boys to cross first, and, as I was one of the youngest, I was one of the first to cross to Gilo 2. Just as when we crossed the Pinyudo, there were few boats, so the process was slow. We waited anxiously on the other side for our friends who were still crossing.

Midday, we heard gunshots. The fire had arrived, and Gilo 1 was under attack. As Salva Kiir Mayardit predicted, the Ethiopian rebels, unhappy with the SPLM, and, therefore, all South Sudanese, followed us to ensure that no Lost Boy remained in Ethiopia. Because of the Ethiopian rebels' alliance with the government in Khartoum, they wished to sever all ties with the Lost Boys. We had become a liability, an unwanted connection to Dr. John Garang. As they opened fire on those who remained, the SPLA soldiers fought to ensure the Lost Boys crossed safely to Gilo 2 before the rebels made the passage into Sudan.

In reaction to the fighting, everyone waiting to be loaded into the boats - men and women, caretakers and Lost Boys - jumped into the churning river. Those who knew how to swim tried to fight the waves to get to Gilo 2, but they struggled against the non-swimmers who clung desperately to their backs for safety. I watched, helpless as the rebels killed those still trying to cross and many others drowned in this river between two lands.

While at Gilo 2, we couldn't wait for those still fighting to arrive, the danger was too great. With our hearts heavy for our friends, we set off for Pochalla, a town bordering Ethiopia but inside the borders of Sudan. Many of the survivors caught up with us as we rushed towards safety, but I was devastated by the loss of the Lost Boys who were killed or drowned as they tried to leave. Fearful for our lives, we walked in haste for another day and a half. While the heat bore down on us, self-preservation drove us onward.

We made it to Pochalla in June 1991, the beginning of

the rainy season. Our arrival was marked with a storm, a deluge that consumed what little we had. We struggled to cover ourselves and what was left of our food; the flour we carried with us from Pinyudo got soaked, and the rain carried much of it away. As Pochalla was now controlled by SPLM/A, the people there welcomed us with joy. They showed us where to settle, and we sat beneath the trees to wait out the storm.

Now back in Sudan, we had to worry about the war between the northern Arabs and native southern tribes. The threat of war loomed all around us, a real and constant danger - we were fugitives in our own land. Two days after our arrival in Pochalla, it, too, fell prey to war. Bombs dropped around us, whistles followed by deafening explosions. With ringing ears, we quickly gathered what little we had and fled again, this time for a site in Golkuur, which, although only about 15 miles away from the town of Pochalla, was thought to be safe from the constant aerial bombardment by Sudan's government.

As we had grown accustomed, we set up temporary makeshift shelters. This transient lifestyle began to gnaw at my soul. My dream of an education began to feel like a distant memory. I tried to retain my focus, to appreciate that I was safe, that my friends were safe, yet as our food supplies emptied, the ravenous, animal hunger left little room to think of anything but the gnawing ache inside my stomach. Once more, I had to resort to scavenging for leaves and wild fruits. I grew despondent as my desperation for food consumed me.

In July 1991, I could no longer bear the hunger and banded together with some of the boys who were also tired of leaves and fruits. The agony of our empty stomachs ruled our rationality. Despite the danger, we decided to return to Pinyudo refugee camp to bring back rations from the deserted food supplies. Determinedly, we walked for two days through a small village called Nyum, an Anyuak village, and reached Chamluong, a small town 45 miles away from Pinyudo. In Chamluong, we ran into a SPLA force, which had just crossed Pinyudo. In our hunger, their warnings of the flooded river washed over us like air. So close to our destination, logic could not reason with our starved stomachs; we could sense the food stores on the other side of the river. Heedless of their cautions, we rushed on past the soldiers and to the river. Finally standing before the Pinyudo, our excitement faltered, as between us and the food stores in Pinyudo refugee camp, stood a flooded river, churning and turbulent. Still our stomachs were our masters. We didn't care about the risks. We were going to make the passage, and we were going to get food.

To our discouragement, a group of SPLA soldiers followed us and ordered us not to cross. Irrational in our starvation, we argued with the soldiers, who pushed us away from the river banks and barred our way. Our protectors became our enemies. In the midst of much confusion, I met another young boy named Awino, who quickly became my friend. Awino, who just returned from Pinyudo, said the Ethiopian rebels had planted land mines all over Pinyudo refugee camp, including the food stores. Like the SPLA, he advised me not to proceed to Pinyudo.

Humbled by the admonitions of the soldiers, we followed them back to the camp, where the SPLA forces, who had brought some food with them from Pinyudo, took pity on us. While their supplies were meager, just what they carried on their heads, they shared their portions of maize and rice with us. Being so starved, these paltry rations did nothing to abate my hunger. I told myself that the soldiers were hoarding the food for themselves; I did not believe the food stores were trapped. I needed to see the stores for myself.

I explored Chamluong looking for a way to bypass the soldiers who blocked the path to Pinyudo, which, in my starvation, I transformed into a mythical sanctuary for food, a place just within and beyond my reach. After wandering about Chamluong for two days with Awino, who had nothing better to do, and the other Lost Boys and making no progress in crossing to Pinyudo, the SPLA force, under captain Aguekdit, ordered everybody to leave. The government soldiers were closing in, and the SPLA had concerns much greater than wrestling with a band of hungry and illogical boys. Together with the SPLA forces, I walked dejectedly back to Pochalla. About midday, the SPLA soldiers ordered us to stop for a meal. They built a fire and proceeded to cook - maize and rice.

Just as we were about to eat our small portions, Anyuak tribesmen attacked us. The rat-a-tat of the gunfire reverberated in my mind and soul, a deathly racket that bore with it the memories of people falling wide-eyed and silent as I fled my village, Ethiopia, Gilo - images blended into one horrific and painful, living stew. Trembling in fear, caught in both past and present, I gripped my ears in an attempt to block out the sounds of death. The SPLA quickly returned the gunfire and killed one of the invaders, but the rest of the assailants, caught off guard, fled.

More than a dozen of our people were killed, including one lady, whom I later discovered to be my distant auntie on my mother's side. We buried our dead in a mass grave and continued our journey. People died, yet we marched on. The blessing of the survivors. Forever marching on.

As a young boy, the deaths of all of these people had a profound affect on me. I couldn't figure out how to just walk away and continue as though nothing happened. As an adult, I still don't understand how to compartmentalize death, yet

I recognize that it is somehow necessary in order to go on living. To dwell in the horrors, to try to apply logic is madness. I also now realize, as I strive to build education in my country, that I can best honor those fallen by not allowing their deaths to be in vain.

After the Anyuak attack, we walked hungry and shaken for two days and arrived in Pochalla on the second evening. The following morning, the soldiers remained in Pochalla while a group of them escorted us to Golkuur Refugee Camp. On our way to the Golkuur, I escaped from the soldiers and returned to Pochalla town. I was desperate for food and even more desperate to find my family. I decided to find someone in Pochalla to take me back to Bor. Young and small in the midst of all of the confusion, I could not find anyone to help me. Dejected, I went and sat under a mango tree. I had no expectations except to sleep under the shade of that tree. I had no food, family, or home, and this tree felt like a good place to be. As I lie beneath the canopy of the mango, I saw my cousin, Kuol Malith Reech, a commander in the SPLA, pass by. I rose and walked to him. I saw concern cross his face, and for a moment he just stared. Then, to my relief, he took me to his home and introduced me into his family.

Kuol's family had little food, yet they welcomed and cared for me. While I greatly appreciated their efforts, being a part of his family made me long even more for my own family. A few weeks after my arrival, Kuol told me he was headed to Bor, my home village. Twelve years old and tired of refugee life, I begged Kuol to take me along so that I could find my family. Kuol agreed.

While I was wearied with walking, this journey filled me with hope. Over and over, I imagined my reunion with my family. Kuol and I began to pack in preparation for the 45 days walk to Bor. I could barely contain my joy and anticipation. Unable to sit still, I bounced all over Kuol's home. "Nathaniel," Kuol's wife admonished, "be still!" knowing as she spoke that her words were futile.

A week before our departure, SPLA soldiers arrived with news that Dr. Riek Machar had mobilized the White Army, a group of Nuer civilian militia from his community, with promises of looting and led an attack on Bor. According to the SPLA soldiers' account, Bor was obliterated—with over three thousand civilians killed, villages burned to ashes, cows looted, and farms destroyed. The Nuer and the Dinka had a history of conflict, and while they initially joined forces to fight against the northern oppression, the tribal differences began to cause conflict within the SPLA ranks. Dr. Riek Machar, a Nuer with a PhD from England, could not agree on the vision of the liberation struggle with Dr. John Garang De Mabior, a Dinka Bor with a PhD from America. Dr. Garang's vision was to fight for all marginalized people of Sudan while Dr. Machar wanted to fight for the independence of South Sudan. Dr. Garang believed that fighting solely in the name of separating South Sudan denied the rights of South Sudanese allies, especially the marginalized people in North Sudan, who could also join in the fight against the Khartoum government. In November 1991, Dr. Machar, claiming a lack of democracy within the SPLM/A movement, formed a breakaway faction of the SPLA called the SPLA-Nasir faction, which consisted of Nuer SPLA soldiers, and orchestrated a coup against Dr. Garang, but SPLA forces loyal to Dr. Garang defeated Machar's men. As a result, Dr. Machar rallied the White Army to fight alongside the SPLA-Nasir army. Failing to topple Dr. Garang militarily, Dr. Machar resorted to beating Dr. Garang into submission by killing Bor civilians—Dr. Garang's community and family.

Devastated over the deaths of "three thousand" civilians in my community, I could not rule out the probability of family being among those massacred, and the that fact my journey home was canceled made this fear even more paralyzing. I was unable to reunite with my family or even learn whether or not they were dead or alive. I cried myself into unconsciousness for days. Kuol counseled me and promised to head home with the SPLA and report back to me with news of our families. We shared our final thoughts and wishes, and Kuol departed for Bor with the SPLA.

I remained a lost child wrestling with life in Pochalla town. Missing my family, I decided to join my friends in Golkuur Refugee Camp. Life grew worse as I again depended on leaves and wild fruits. In August 1991, four months after our flight from Ethiopia, the United Nations began food drops. While the small rations of beans, lentils, and rice did little to abate our hunger, we were no longer starving. Kwashakwar and Claire of International Committee of the Red Cross (ICRC) flew into Pochalla from Kenya to help with the camp organization and to ensure our care. Without our stomachs as our masters, we began to rebuild our fractured lives again. We built makeshift homes and schools. The SPLA provided us with teachers, and our education resumed.

In April of 1992, just as we began to feel settled, the SPLA intercepted news that government troops were advancing toward Pochalla, and, soon after this news, Sudan's government started to bomb us. With the sky again raining fire, the SPLM leadership ordered us out of Pochalla. Many Lost Boys were killed or injured during this attack. My friend and cousin John Anyaak was shot and injured in this attack. The UN transported him to Lopiding Hospital in Lokichoggio, Kenya, along with the other injured. By the time

John made it to the hospital, it was too late to save his leg, yet he miraculously survived.

Not everyone was strong enough to make the journey. Due to the meager rations and close living quarters, there were many sick people who couldn't walk and had to remain in Golkuur. My friend, Achieh Anyang, a leader of our group, was among the sick. I later learned that, a week after we left, Sudanese government forces overran the SPLA and captured Pochalla. They killed most of the sick and took the rest to Khartoum. My friend was among those taken to Khartoum.

Those who were able to walk were ordered to leave. Again, I prepared to walk. The SPLA assigned two SPLA officers, Mayen Ngor and Machut Baarach, to lead us out of Pochalla and into Kenya. Sudan was no longer safe. As the journey would prove treacherous, the SPLA provided our teachers with guns for additional protection. With the armed teachers and a small SPLA contingent as an escort, we abruptly left Pochalla. Again I walked.

While I dreaded the never-ending walking, I felt that this journey was different. On our last journey we fled alone and without direction; this time Kwashakwar and Claire of the ICRC remained with us, and their presence provided an element of safety. They led and followed us with their Toyota Land Cruisers and at least two trucks of food, and, while we were still exhausted and hungry, we had rations of beans and rice. Although these rations seemed meager with our continued exertion, on this journey, we had something to eat beyond leaves and berries.

Under the leadership of Mayen and Machut, we walked—they determined when we rested and when we moved. Kwashakwar and Claire tried to carry as many of the weak as they could in their vehicles, yet they only had two trucks - there were hundreds of us. In a spirit of camaraderie, we comforted one another; we bound each other's wounds, we shared food and water, we buried our dead, and the elder boys carried the refugees too weak to walk. While we tried to push each other onward, many of the evacuees who, weakened by thirst and hunger, lagged behind and fell prey to lions and unfriendly local tribes. We all tried to huddle into the center of our groups, as we knew that our predators were picking off those who walked on the outside.

We walked through Pakok, Nyalongoro and eventually climbed the Boma mountains. Exhausted and hungry, this climb sapped our strength. I remember using the peak as a marker. I kept telling myself that once I reached that peak, the hardest part of the journey would be over. With this thought in mind, I pushed myself to keep up with the others. Once I reached the elusive top of this mountain, I collapsed into a collective heap with the other boys. I could not go on; none of us could. That night, having conquered a mountain, I slept a dreamless sleep, the soundest sleep I had in months. The next morning the journey continued.

It seemed to me as though I would be forever walking. I walked in the day, in the night and in my dreams. For two months, I was a body that walked, ate, slept, and walked some more. Sometimes we stopped for a few hours, sometimes for the night, and when I wasn't resting, I walked.

One morning, we started to walk, and as the sun reached its fiery apex, we came to a place called Koor Agreb, which translates as Scorpion Stream. Named for its poisonous inhabitants, Koor Agreb, the stream teemed with scorpions, to us, was life giving. We drank deep, reviving gulps. The sun burned with intensity, so, exhausted from the heat and sated with the waters, we rested, heedless of our poisonous companions.

Ahead of us loomed a huge desert called Kasengor, an obstacle to our intended destination, Magoos, where the UN had set up temporary tents and food storage. Seeing the heat waves rippling over the desert like moving waters, our leaders and Kwashakwar and Claire decided that we would spend the night in Khoor Agreb. We drank, cooked, and slept in this place of the scorpions.

Early the next morning, trucks sent by ICRC arrived, yet there still weren't enough trucks to carry all of us across the Kasengor. Our leaders squeezed the youngest boys into the trucks and told the older boys to begin to cross the desert while it was still cold. Being younger, I boarded one of the trucks. The trucks dropped us off at Magoos and quickly returned to get the boys who walked. The trucks collected the heat-scorched boys who faltered in the middle of Kasengor desert and returned with them to Magoos. As the older boys climbed off of the trucks, I felt a surge of relief. We lost no one else; we had all made it to Magoos safely.

In Magoos, the ICRC again set up to feed us. We went to the food stores to collect our rations. We again began to settle and gather our strength, but after only two days, the Jie community, inhabitants of the area, thought we were there to occupy their land. Through its divide and conquer strategy, the Khartoum government fed many local tribes the propaganda that the Dinka were the reason for the suffering in the country since the Dinka had initiated the rebellion against the government in Khartoum. As most of us were Dinka, the Jie community thought we had come to their land with conflict. The Jie tribesmen attacked us as we slept. I awoke to the explosion of gunshots and ran—dodging bullets in the night. As the Jie shot indiscriminately into the crowd, several friends fell around me. I heaved with fear and anger.

The ICRC hurriedly moved to escape. Again, the trucks

loaded the youngest first, and I boarded one of the trucks. The trucks carried us through Kapoeta all the way to Narus, a town on the Sudan and Kenyan border. They unloaded us and returned to get the older boys. These boys, our friends, had already walked from Magoos to Kapoeta - a distance of two days. They were loaded into the trucks and transported to Narus to join us.

A few weeks later, Kapoeta also fell to the Khartoum government. We had to run to Kenya. We walked for a day to Lokichoggio, a Kenyan town just over the border. After a week in Lokichoggio, more trucks arrived, enough to carry all of the Lost Boys, and the ICRC transported us to Kakuma Refugee Camp. After three months of walking, I was arriving to yet another home.

Chapter Five: Welcome to Kenya

At last we stopped. We had reached our destination. Corpses of camels, donkeys, cows, goats, sheep, dogs, and people greeted us. At thirteen years of age, I had grown accustomed to seeing death, to smelling death, to confronting death, yet, faced with this eviron of mass death, I fell to my knees, my mind and body numb. Through this fog, I heard a voice say that we had reached Kakuma, Kenya, a northeastern town inhabited by the nomadic tribe, the Turkana.

Here, in this desert place, the acacia blew its natural whistle, the sun ruled the day with its sweltering heat, dust ruled the ground, sand storms ruled the air; water was scarce, and no Turkana dared to farm. Due to the continuous sand storms, UN vehicles drove with their headlights on during the day. This no-man's land was Kakuma, Kenya - my new home.

Except for the UN presence, Kakuma was a duplicate of Pinyudo refugee camp. We wasted no time resuming the way of life to which we had grown accustomed. As in Pinyudo, we went about reestablishing our makeshift shelters. Exhausted from the journey, I, along with my fellow Lost Boys, helped the others gather sticks, and once more, we built our shelters out of small poles, sacks, leaves, and the UN donated plastic sheets we had carried on our trek to Kakuma. While this was to be my home, I felt discouraged in its sense of impermanence. With this second flight to yet another place of transient dwellings, I felt like a blown-about weed. I missed my home. I missed my family.

Soon after we completed these crude shelters that would serve as our homes, we again started classes under the trees. I worked hard and completed Class four. In 1993, however, the UN and Kenyan authorities declared that we should receive a more formal education with more qualified teachers, so we repeated Class four inside the brick and corrugated iron sheet classrooms of Raja Primary school in Kakuma refugee camp. However, we now had new Kenyan teachers and so had a new curriculum. Arabic was dropped, and I now had to learn Kiswahili alongside English, so at times I felt overwhelmed. Yet the languages and the new knowledge thrilled me. With these more rigorous studies, I felt a rekindling of hope, a lifting of my spirits, as I had grown to love learning. I drank it in like parched soil, and my confidence began to return.

With food for the mind, body, and soul, Kakuma served as a considerable refuge. The United Nations ensured that water wells were built and that food was delivered every month - maize, wheat flour, oil, beans, and lentils. They parceled out small rations of food for which I was entirely grateful. I did not have to scavenge for my existence in this desert place. The food was not enough, but I was able to eat at least twice every day.

Soon, however, Kakuma started to fill up with more refugees, escapees from Congo, Rwanda, Somalia, Ethiopia, Burundi, Uganda, and Sudan. The upsurge forced the United Nations to cut the quantity of rations in an attempt to provide food to everyone. In response to this influx of people, the UN changed the method of food distribution. Instead of delivery to the groups, the UN started to build barbed wire fences with cages on the inside. These fences served as our new food distribution centers. The idea incensed every refugee - no one wanted to receive food in the wired cage like an animal. We demonstrated daily in an attempt to keep the UN from building fences. For about three months, the UN built fences in the day, and we tore them down in the night.

Having lost control of the situation, the UN sought the

aid of the Kenyan police. The police had no mercy, and the battle grew brutal. Many people died in the fight against the police. Eventually, we conceded, and the ration distribution proceeded as planned - in the cages inside the fences. Every month, everyone went to the distribution centers to receive food--a monthly supply of four cups of flour, two cups of beans, one cup of oil, and two tablespoons of salt. When I arrived in the United States, much later, I felt shocked and outraged to discover how household pets received more food than we had received in the camps, more than what many refugees still receive today. The food we were given in Kenya was not enough for a pet, yet in our refugee world, it sustained our lives.

I figured this food was not going to last a month if I cooked alone, so my friends and I devised a concept of partnership. We pooled our food together, and began to economize and cook in schedules. This way, we were able to eat once a day, or at least every other day, and our food lasted over three weeks and ran out just a few days before we were to receive our next rations.

In this world of dust and death, our scarce food supplies became a source of conflict. The Turkana, who were also starving, began to raid us nightly for food. Their raiding methods were random. They demanded food at gunpoint, shooting whoever refused them; they shot people through the windows and then broke into their shelters to collect food; they attacked people in the evening, while people still chatted outside of their compounds. I lived in fear of these raids that came at any time - day, evening, and night. These food raids resulted in the injuries and deaths of many of the Lost Boys.

Our refugee camp gradually turned into a battleground for our food and lives. My classmate Daniel Yor Deng was paralyzed by a bullet. I lost my pastor Majok Tuil, my basketball coach Manyuon Kuol Ayuen, my uncle-in-law Majak Alier Agou, and many other mentors and friends. Captive by this constant threat, we lived a mundane life and believed in an inconsequential future. As South Sudan was just miles away, most of my fellow Lost Boys of Sudan decided it was time to go back to fight for the liberation of South Sudan. They could not stay to die a desperate death in a forsaken refugee camp so they left to join the Sudan People's Liberation Army. It was here that Peter Anyieth left me.

"Nathaniel," Peter began, "I must join the fight. I can no longer sit and watch as more and more of our people suffer and die."

Immediately, I stood to go with him, but, once more, he assumed the role of my father. "Nathaniel, you are young. You must go to school," Peter urged.

"Peter, no!" I implored. "I'm coming with you." I couldn't bear the thought of losing someone else close to me. Peter had been my closest friend since Reech died in Pinyudo. It was Peter who had watched over me, Peter who had saved me.

"I am not asking," Peter asserted kindly yet firmly. "You are smart. You will help by going to school."

Reluctantly, I heeded his advice, and the desperate refugee camp life became a part of me. I felt my newly quenched soul begin to wither.

Once, as I waited in the cage for my ration of food, a refugee in front cried out, "What is this? This food wouldn't feed a tsetse fly!"

The UN volunteer looked at the boy coldly, shrugged and stated, "Beggars can't be choosers."

As I struggled to survive, physically and mentally, in Kakuma, that volunteer's words replayed in my mind again and again. Forced to rely on a foreign government for food in this foreign land, I felt very much like a beggar. I realized that, for my health and my potential future, I had to be my own change, to strive for my education. I chose to rise above my beggarly and inconsequential existence, and in the name of this elusive education, I surrendered to the enslaving life of Kakuma refugee camp and left the rest to God.

The tensions of the camp continued. Each day was a battle for life. Seeing the faltering morale of the students, the UN and teachers of Raja Primary school collaborated to organize a football team. Eagerly, I went to the tryouts and made the Raja Primary School football (Soccer) team. The first day I entered the field, an announcer, who didn't know my real name, nicknamed me *Makandeer*, a Dinka word for a skinny but determined individual. Another boy, David Kiir Awan became my partner and, later, my best friend. He was an offensive midfielder, and I was a defensive midfielder.

Our primary school soon began to dominate the high school leagues. In late 1993, the director of sport, Madong William Mading, in consultation with James Njoroge, education camp manager for Save the Children Sweden, recruited Abraham Ajhok Kuol, my distant cousin and our goalkeeper, and my friend David and I as part of a Sudanese refugee football team to represent Kakuma in a district football competition in Lodwar, the capital of Turkana district. We won that title and headed to a regional competition in Kapenguria, the capital of West Pokot district, where we also won the regional title. From Kapenguria, we headed to Nakuru, the capital of Rift Valley province to compete for the Provincial Cup. We lost in the quarter finals. However, we played a strong game and went far together in competition - it was exhilarating.

For me, football served as more than just an enjoyable

sport; it was my escape from refugee life. Running on the field, I was no longer a refugee, but a talented human being. I soared; I was limitless. After my return to Kakuma, I continued to play soccer for my school, and to this day, football remains a part of me.

While football invigorated and freed me, education quenched my soul. I continued to throw myself into my studies. I wanted to learn everything I could, and I realized that the more I learned the more I had to learn. Knowledge, for me, was a journey. In 1997, I sat for the Kenyan Certificate for Primary Education (KCPE), the examination that marks the completion of the eighth grade. I scored 388 out 700 points. To my frustration, I missed a UN scholarship to study in a Kenyan high school by 12 points and was instead admitted to Napata Secondary School, a UN run high school. Two years later, I transferred to Bortown Secondary School, also a UN run high school. This school, a cool gray structure of concrete and iron, lacked books and qualified teachers; still, I was determined to learn and I studied everything presented to me.

While I pursued my education, I joined three football clubs, a junior refugee camp team and two local clubs, Bor Bright Star and Jalle Invincible Heroes. My football skills broadened. I became a talented and aggressive striker, a leading scorer, and a strong passer. My refugee camp team beat many Kenyan teams, and my two local teams did equally as well. As we defeated many competitors, our games gained attention in the camp. Despite hunger and difficulty, people began to converge to watch the games. The football field became a palace of consolation.

People grew excited with the way we played and began to pick teams to support. Every weekend, the refugees arrived in droves to cheer for their favorite teams. We brought smiles and happiness to their gloomy faces, a light into the darkness of the camps. Our games became a therapy for stress and hunger - for us and for our fans. With the excitement our game incited among the refugees, I realized I was part of a group that entertained suffering souls, and I pushed harder to master my game, and I did. I became renown in the camps, a status that earned me another nickname among my fans - Ability, meaning a capable individual. I still go by this nickname, as it reminds me of my capacity to both grow as an individual and to raise the spirits of others.

Chapter Six: The Call to Adventure

In 1998, at age 19, I was grown and ready to look for a girl partner. Since more refugees joined us in the camp, there were now Sudanese girls in the camp. However, I found many obstacles to finding a girl. I had never dated. I was shy and lacked confidence, and, even with my fame in the camps as a football player, I still lived the desperate life of a Lost Boy, and no parent would welcome a lost youth, a source of hunger, into a family.

Even with my orphan status, I believed I was different. I was a popular football star and a student with a positive attitude and an ambition to succeed. I disregarded all the negatives and began my search for a girl. One day, at a traditional Dinka Bor dance, I saw a girl, young but beautiful, in a purple shirt and skirt that highlighted her slender figure. With her smooth, high forehead, ebony skin, and warm, thoughtful eyes, she possessed an elegant grace I had never before seen in a girl or a woman. I wanted to speak to her, but, as a part of the Dinka traditional norms, I couldn't speak to her at the dance. An unknown man approaching an underage girl in a public setting could cause problems for her within the community. I couldn't wait for the occasion to end.

Finally, after spending the evening full of tortured curiosity, I furtively followed her home. Shy and scared, I squeaked a pitiful, "What's your name?"

"Yar Mayom," she answered timidly.

"Yar," I thought to myself, "Of course. She is the great white cow." I was enthralled.

In keeping with tradition, I didn't tell her I was interested because she was young. I instead went to my cousin Akuak Deng Mayen for more research. Luckily, my cousin was related to her and advised me to consult Yar's older cousin Ajoh Alier Agou.

As directed, I went to her cousin. In preparation for this meeting, I had my hair cut, my shoes shined, and dressed in my best clothing. In courtship, appearances are everything. To the Dinka, attitude and appearance are what initially determines worth. If the family and the girl like a man's appearance, they then do their research to learn about his character. I wanted my appearance and confidence to win Yar's heart. In my nervousness, I fell short of words, but, in this first and necessary step, I managed to introduce myself to her cousin. Skipping the traditional formal introductions and small talk, I skipped straight to the point. "I am in love with your cousin Yar," I blurted out bluntly. Amusement lit her features, as, with arched eyebrows, she eyed me from head to toe. I had to swallow the lump that formed in my throat during this scrutiny.

After this speedy summation and an excruciating pause, her cousin nodded her approval. She welcomed me to the family, pending a final approval from Yar herself. She was the one who had the final say. This approval bolstered my flagging confidence. I had passed my first test.

On my next visit, I went to visit Yar with my cousins. Yar's cousin, with a group of her other cousins, welcomed us home. Together, we engaged introductions, and I was formally introduced to Yar. Then an informal bargain ensued. We all approved of the engagement, but Yar and I were encouraged to meet alone, so on the official visit, Yar's cousin, as part of the Dinka norm, stepped outside to give Yar and me some privacy. I told Yar that she was beautiful and that I would like to be engaged to her. I nervously hoped that Yar, too, approved of my looks and that my confident attitude would win her heart. Young and naïve, Yar reciprocated my love with a smile. She neither approved nor disapproved, but she welcomed my visitations, and whenever I had time, I paid her a visit by appointment.

A simple mannered, wise, faithful, and traditional girl with solid reputation and a good sense of her identity, Yar possessed qualities that endeared her to many youth. I was not the only boy in love with her. Relations in our culture between boys and girls are not girlfriend and boyfriend relations but potential fiancé-fiancée relations, and it was a stiff competition. According to tradition, each of Yar's suitors was given equal access. I didn't care. I promised to court her with respect and devotion. I had confidence in my abilities, but I was anxious with worry. By all means, I'm a handsome young man, but I'm not the handsomest. I'm six feet tall, but in a society where men could be six feet, nine inches to over seven feet, I'm short. Dinka women tend to appreciate such attributes, and my self-esteem faltered. As a Lost Boy without any family to aid me in my search for a mate, I had to act as my own salesman.

When I visited Yar, her sisters welcomed me, and Yar and I were left alone in a room to share our romantic thoughts, but with limitations. In respect to myself, Yar, and Dinka tradition, I could initiate a conversation with love and end it with love to convince her I was her right lover, but we were not allowed to touch. Finally, after about two years of courtship, I gained Yar's love. She said, "Gentle man, you are considerate. You gave me a chance for flexibility, and I think you are a responsible young man and could be a responsible husband." I was perplexed. I didn't know I possessed a gift of courtship, and my heart swelled with joy and pride.

I was happy to have won the love of my life, but according to Dinka culture, the next challenge now was to win my family's blessings to approach Yar's family for a marriage proposal, but I had no family in the refugee camp, only my friends and cousins. Another challenge was, at 5'8", Yar, like me, was not that tall, but she was beautiful and rich in qualities that, to the Dinka, overshadow stature. My friends approved of our union, but I worried if, when I was reunited with my family, they would accept her.

Yar also didn't have her biological family in the camp, yet she came from a renowned family; her grandfather served as an officer in Anyanya One, the war for the liberation of South Sudan, and in the camps she had her sisters and a network of foster uncles and mothers who looked out for her well-being.

Now that Yar had accepted me as her choice, I needed the approval of Yar's network of family. I approached them with confidence and was immediately deflated. The first question I was asked was, "How will you care for our daughter?"

"I plan to study and get a good job," I responded.

"What are you going to do now?" an uncle asked.

"Ummm… I will get my diploma and a good job," I responded.

"And until then?" was the response.

I loved Yar, but that's not what Yar's family wanted to hear. To them, my love alone was not enough. A huge obstacle suddenly mounted itself between our love. As she is of status and wealth, her family hoped for a dowry and demanded many cows - no less than 100 cows. As a Lost Boy, I held no status, and I had no cows.

Despite these challenges, Yar and I decided to become engaged. We completely believed, and continue to believe, that God thought we were made for each other.

I was becoming a man. A girl, a beautiful, kind girl, had chosen me. I knew the rest would come. I was elated.

Just after Yar chose me to be her husband, I heard news

that the International Committee of the Red Cross (ICRC) had established a correspondence between the Sudanese refugees in Kenya and the Sudanese in hiding in the jungle of Sudan. Mixed with trepidation and hope, I went to the ICRC. After eleven years of separation from my family, without knowing whether my family was alive or dead, I sent them a letter with my picture attached, and the ICRC personnel worked to locate my family.

Soon, I held a letter from my mother in my hand. With shaking hands, I opened the letter and read my mother's words. "My prayers," she wrote, "are answered. We thought you were dead; however, we refrained from any memorial service, as we were waiting to receive definite news about you. Your siblings and I live along the river Nile, not far from where you left us. We hid in the papyrus reeds during the war. Dear son, with my heart filled with grief, I regret to report to you that your father died in the early 90s. In God, we have hoped that one day, we shall be reunited. Do not be overtaken by the news of your father's death and our situation," she warned. "Keep us in your daily prayers."

The news bothered me for days. I couldn't psychologically process that my father; my mentor, friend, and role model, was gone. My mother and siblings, who were miraculously alive, were somewhere in the unknown. A part of my heart thought it would be better to quit school and go to Sudan to join the Sudan People's Liberation Army in an effort to find my family. The other part of my heart said, "What are you going to give them? The only hope for them now is your education. After high school, there is a high chance of returning to your family with a great gift." My two hearts argued for months. Eventually, the second heart won. Education, I decided, was my father and mother for the time. I concluded that I must complete high school and then look for my family afterward.

    My future lay before me, full of possibilities. I had a beautiful fiancée, my mother was alive, and I was pursuing an education. Yet a cloud of turmoil, heavy and churning, brewed within me. I made my choice for education; now, I had to succeed. Failure was not an option. My mother, my brothers and my future with Yar depended on me. So I fought back my own self-doubt and my fears for my family and began each day with renewed effort. In this daily shadow battle with myself, I pushed towards a purpose I was just beginning to understand more fully. I studied to be worthy of Yar; I studied to save my family; for the sake of knowledge, I studied.

PART TWO: A JOURNEY TO A NEW LAND

"I must study politics and war that my sons may have liberty to study mathematics and philosophy."

~ John Adams

Chapter Seven: A Piece of Luck is Better Than Knowledge

Unexpectedly, just as I needed to prove my worth to Yar's family and to myself, another door of opportunity opened. When I was in school in Kenya, my teachers told a story to encourage my classmates and me in our studies and prepare us for the competitive nature of education and advancement. The power of this story, of the harsh nature of fortune out of misfortune, still dominates my mind: "Once upon a time, a certain boy was attending high school. One day, he sat for his high school certificate. He passed the exam. However, a certain number was required in order to make the list of government-sponsored students to university. He missed the list by one person. He was devastated. Unfortunately for one family, the school, and the rest of the students, but fortunately for him, one of the sponsored boys suddenly died before the university opened. In order to present a complete list to the university, the government officials came back for one student, and since he was on top of the list, he was sponsored and admitted to the university. Upon graduating from college, he wrote a book entitled *A Piece of Luck is better than Knowledge.*" I heard this story and hoped for that bit of "luck" for myself, but I had no idea what luck I was hoping for; I just longed for a change in circumstance and possessed a vague hope for a future I could not yet see beyond the purgatory of the camp.

While in my home village, before my world was consumed by flames, we occasionally saw airplanes as we played. Some of the large airplanes formed long smoke-like trails, white curling wisps in a blue sky, that we thought looked like tails. Whenever we saw one of these tails, we would run beneath the plane and yell, "America! America!

America!" To me, the plane was America. I had no idea what America was, that it was a country in a foreign land. To me, "America" was the smoky-tail-trail of an airplane. My village was my world, and I didn't know the world extended so far beyond my familiar boundaries, so I never desired to leave for some far-off place.

I continued to see the world through the lenses of my village in the refugee camp in Kenya. I never dreamed of America. All I wanted was to go home once the war was over and be reunited with my family. Committed to finishing high school, getting a job, finding my family, and getting married, I pushed on. The United Nations, my other family, had different plans for me. One of the plans was to resettle the "Lost Boys of Sudan," the group I became associated with, somewhere in a developed nation to begin a new life. Personnel at the UN headquarters realized that Lost Boys of Sudan were graduating from high school in Kakuma Refugee Camp and that none were working or attending college. These statistics led the United Nations to shop for a country to resettle us. The United States of America immediately offered that opportunity for a lucky few, but with one requirement - a personal autobiography. The U.S government wanted to first determine our potential for success.

In 1998, without disclosing a reason, the United Nations' Save the Children Sweden personnel took passport-sized photographs of us and asked us to write autobiographies. We responded as requested. For us, each new development was a chance to perhaps get new resources in the camp. In 2000, it turned out we were being prepared to go to America, but only if we did well in our interviews. Through Sudanese caregivers, who were employed by the United Nations as our stand-in guardians, we were told to get ready for the American immigration lawyers who were coming to interview us. The questions covered the Sudan Civil War; how we left home, what we experienced, saw, and felt, and why we wanted to go to America.

I spoke to Yar about this opportunity, and she gave me her unfailing encouragement. She saw it as an opportunity for me but also as an opportunity for us. If I was chosen for resettlement, I would gain status in her family's eyes; I would become worthy to marry Yar.

The interview began with the underage refugees, those who were under 18 years of age and considered dependents. They were to stay with American families as foster children. The underage Lost Boys who passed the interview were flown to America in 2000. For the older boys, we were advised to group with our best friends so that we could afford lives in America. I teamed up with my long time friends and group mates Gabriel Gai Magok, Awino Gam Day, Santino Mawei Garang, Abraham Madit Nhiany, and my distant cousin John Anyaak, who had lost his leg during the Arab attack on Pochalla. My cousin, John Anyaak, however, was not in our group, so I introduced him to the other boys, and because of their profound trust in me, they welcomed him to our new family. With our freshly forged family intact, we were ready for our interviews.

During my interview, I told the lawyer that I wanted to go to America to start a new life. I further emphasized that, "I needed to make money, to go to school, to find my family, and to help my country."

After writing briefly on my file, he smiled at me, and said, "Wait for the result. Good luck."

The lawyer's two impersonally spoken words, "Good luck," crushed me with the weight of a mountain and the sinking stone of fear settled heavy in my stomach. I thought I had failed the interview.

After four long weeks, my friends and I were finally called to the United Nations Kakuma's compound for the results. We had already heard the devastating outcome of some of the failed interviews and were frightened of news that killed as mightily as a gun. Some of the boys who were interviewed before us had unsuccessful interviews and, as a result, some had committed suicide. They viewed their failures as a life sentence in the camps and gave up hope. Bearing a desperate desire to rise above the cruel and monotonous nothingness of the refugee camps, my friends and I nervously went to learn our fates, to find out if we were deemed worthy by a foreign government to live in a foreign land, whether we were to be offered a new beginning or be condemned to the hollowed life of a refugee, somewhere between existence and nonexistence. Afraid of ourselves, we went to hear the results with a plan to comfort each other in case we were not chosen. As names were being read out, I waited and waited ... and waited, the rock heavy twisting inside me.

Finally, the man read, "Nathaniel Chol Nyok."

Enveloped in a heavy silence, I walked toward him with faltering steps. As I fearfully extended my hand to receive my envelope, my hands shook as though the whole ground trembled. I physically could not extend my hands further than elbow length in front of me. Failure and success were suddenly equally terrifying. In silent understanding, Gabriel bravely collected the envelope out of the man's outstretched hand for me. My heart throbbed heavily as Gabriel gently bore this document, this decider of fates, as we both waited for his name to be called.

Then, the man called his name. "Gabriel Gai Magok."

As he had for me, I stepped forward and took the envelope on his behalf. I could scarcely breathe as the faceless man called each of my groupmates' names and each received his envelope. After the catalogue of names had been called, we silently walked to a quiet area. Counseled by our friends, we promised to be calm no matter what happened. A hush fell upon our group as Gabriel and I opened our documents at the same time. In disbelief, I slowly raised my eyes to his and knew he, too, had been chosen. We both gasped for breath before we shouted out our news. "America!" we screamed in unison. My group mates, with trembling hands, hurriedly tore into their envelopes. We were each chosen to resettle in the United States of America under section 207 of the United States immigration code. Although we did not fully understand the implications of this opportunity, we knew that something momentous had just happened to us. The letters marked both a beginning and an end, and we stood in overwhelmed silence, staring blankly at the weighty papers that now dangled limply from our hands. The shock was short-lived, and a new hope coursed through my veins.

This news gave me wings. I felt as though I could soar with those trails in the sky I once thought of as America. But I was going to America, an actual place in a new land. With one sheet of paper, I was offered a new beginning, a way out of the banality of my quotidian existence. While I had no cows to give to Yar's family, it was as though God provided me an answer, an opportunity to go to the United States. I raced to tell Yar the news. As America was known as a land of good fortune, this turn-of-events made me appealing to her family in terms of providing a dowry. They knew their daughter would be cared for, and I was accepted to be the future husband of Yar. We were now, in the eyes of our family, officially engaged.

My friends and I were soon scheduled for medical checks and cultural orientation instruction. We completed every step successfully. Because I was not a teenager, I was considered independent, not dependent. This meant I couldn't stay with an American family as foster child. The cost of my journey and my success in the United States rested on me alone. I signed a Promissory Note, a promise to repay the International Organization for Migration (IOM) for my ticket. With all of the prerequisites completed, I was ready to leave Kakuma at any hour. Every morning, I anxiously visited the board to check for my name. A few long weeks later, my name appeared on the board. I was scheduled to fly to the United States of America.

Now came the hard part. The idea of flying to the United States, farther away from my family, was sickening in its loneliness. While I didn't know whether my family was even alive, I believed in my heart they were close. My original plan was to graduate from high school in Kenya, marry Yar, and head home to find my family. Instead, this new design carried me further away from Sudan. For days, I couldn't sleep as I grappled with the weight of this life decision. I was told that going to America would open opportunities that could change my life for the better. On the other hand, going to Sudan to find my family had been in the forefront of my mind for the past fourteen years.

As I struggled with this choice, I succumbed to exhaustion and dreamed of the story *A Piece of Luck is better than Knowledge*. I believe that this dream came to me as an answer to my dilemma. I realized my journey to America, a land I had never dreamed of, was in sight and full of opportunities for me, my family, and even my country. Just as in my teacher's story, my new knowledge brought me "luck." A new door had opened to me, and it was up to me to enter into this new realm of possibility.

On June 2, 2001 I walked on unsteady legs, both frightened and anxious, to the plane waiting in the dusty field for me and my friends. I was going to soar with the tails. Hundreds of our friends came to see us off, waving their arms and shouting their farewells. Yar, now my fiancée, came to bid me farewell. I did not wish to part from her. I promised her that I would work hard for her, and she promised to wait for me. The oceans separate Africa and America, but they would not part Yar and I. I would return for her. She was in my heart.

One by one, our names were called, and we entered the plane. With my head bent down, I waved a final, tearful goodbye to Yar and my friends. Upon seeing me climbing the stairs to the plane, my soccer fans shouted, "Ability! Ability! Ability!" While I had been so anxious to leave my stifling refugee life behind, it was hard to leave behind the friends I stayed with for more than a decade, yet I was confident that I had made the right decision. I boarded a small plane from Kakuma to Nairobi Kenya for my first flight ever. I knew that as soon as I entered the plane that my life would forever change. The doors to the plane closed, and a new door, both foreign and unimaginable, opened. The flight attendant made sure we were safely buckled into our seats. This was the moment. Our plane taxied away as we continued to bid farewell to our friends through the windows. The plane took off as we watched our friends, the dusty airfield, the camp, and our old lives recede into the distance.

As soon as we were in the air, my friend, Juuk Chaw, looked down, and joked, "What if it falls now?"

In our nerves, we all shouted at him to keep quiet. Thankfully, the plane did not fall, and we made it to Nairobi through the turbulence. At Nairobi's Gold Center, we were given some anti-malaria and deworming medicine and stayed for two days. Drowsy and nervous, we were exposed to the very first cold of a modern town. The brisk air matched the chill of the pavement, concrete, and crowds. Everything moved so quickly, and in spite of us, that I felt elated and small. My heartbeat pulsed to the rhythm of the whirring vehicles, and my step was short and quick as I absorbed the lights and buildings that towered all around me.

On June 4, 2001 I boarded a Saudi Arabian Airline to Jeddah, Saudi Arabia. Shortly after takeoff, the pilot alerted everybody to get ready for landing. We looked at the primary flight display and noticed that Jeddah was not far from Sudan. Fear seeped through my bones as the plane landed just miles away from Khartoum, Sudan. My friends and I thought we were being handed over to the Sudanese government. The fear, thankfully, was an illusion; no such handover happened and our journey continued.

I then flew to Rome, Italy, then to JFK, New York. I spent my first night in America, the night of June 4, 2001 in a Courtyard Marriott in New York. The spacious room, the plush beds, the numerous pillows and the running water all gave me pause. As I stood in disbelief in the center of this luxury, my refugee life seemed even more primitive, and for the first time since I fled that night fourteen years ago, I felt human.

The next morning we were driven to La Guardia Airport for our next flight. We boarded a Delta flight, briefly landed in Washington, D.C., and finally, after six flights across three continents, we arrived in Atlanta. At the gate, we were met by Matthew Ucheng Kon, our case manager from the International Rescue Committee (IRC), a resettlement agency. He held up a sign that had our names and "Welcome to Atlanta" printed in bold, black letters. With just our International Organization for Migration's paper bags, we didn't need to go to the baggage claim. Matthew Kon, through the IRC, rented an apartment for us in Clarkston, Georgia; however, it was not yet ready, so he drove us to a Super 8 Motel on Church Street in Decatur, GA where we spent about three days.

This new and anonymous room, also abound with unfamiliar luxuries, served as my induction to my new home. As I sat in this place, yet another transitional place that was not yet mine, I felt such hope. The stark walls with the singular painting of a floral scene, the two double beds, the coffee pot that spat foul-smelling tar-like liquid, the floor-to-ceiling window that overlooked a street filled with cars that looked like tiny ants moving purposefully below, and the people who walked with resolute haste, all struck me in their complex simplicity. I felt overwhelmed and exhilarated, and a little frightened, to be a part of this bustle and rush of life. I grew dizzy looking down upon the scene below me. No longer was I drifting in a holding place. A place of make-shift houses and meager meals doled out sparingly. I was now in a place that was preparing me for my home.

Home. After so many years in the camps, the word still elicited the pain of memory, yet here I was, a survivor who now had a bed, blankets, and modern conveniences that still felt foreign to me and about to embark on a new beginning. Looking at the tiny people walking with purposeful strides to their destinations, I was excited to race down to join their steady march. I had arrived to a destination, a place where I, too, would have meaning. I vowed to live up to that promise, to work toward building my education and helping my people in the place forever stamped upon my heart, South Sudan, my home.

After three days of exploring and learning my new city, full of harried people and shops with such infinite choices that I often found it difficult to make a decision, our apartment was ready. We were ready to move into our new home. I buzzed with excitement. "Finally," I thought. "Finally."

Chapter Eight: A New Land

Clarkston, Georgia, a city east of Atlanta, which now houses a population of about 8000 residents, 6000 of them foreigners, became my new home in the U.S., where I first lived under the wing of the International Rescue Committee (IRC) for almost three months. They found us a two-bedroom apartment, but, to our dismay, it only fit four of us. John, Abraham, Santino and I were to share an apartment, while our other two friends, Awino and Gabriel, had to live with another group of Lost Boys, who had been accepted into the U.S. like us. Being separated from my friends terrified me. While they were housed in the same apartment complex, the separation felt as though a limb, a part of me was severed. We had all remained together through Pinyudo and Kakuma, and my friends had become an extension of myself, as integral to me as air.

I walked into this apartment with John, Abraham, and Santino and was overtaken by its vastness. Like the hotel, the walls were white, barren, and cold. I shivered from the chill of the air conditioner. Debbie Meyers, our IRC volunteer, showed us where we would sleep. We would share a bedroom, and each of the rooms was equipped with a bunkbed and a dresser for our belongings. She then explained how to adjust the thermostat and showed us how to operate the oven and stovetop. Kindly, our pantry had been stocked with boxes of cereal, jars of peanut butter, and cans of soup. Debbie left and told us she would return in a couple days.

When Debbie left, my friends and I all stood in silence. We had been eagerly awaiting the moment we would move into our new home, yet everything felt so strange and new. In our rush to move, we had not yet eaten so decided we would try to cook some soup as we had been shown. While

Debbie had taught us how to operate the stove, we could not figure out how to open the cans, so we ate the peanut butter and cereal for the first couple of days until she returned. At first, she looked at us in dismay. She then shook her head and laughed at her oversight of this technicality over, what seemed to her, such an ordinary contraption.

As part of our indoctrination into American culture, Debbie advised us to stay away from strangers. She cautioned that we do not get involved in any fight, or accept to sell anything for anybody. The advice frightened and overwhelmed me. I was used to living in a community that worked together, and to helping someone in need of assistance. While there were a few people who made trouble in the camps, I didn't understand this lesson to mistrust people unfamiliar to me, and I was afraid of making a mistake.

One day, about a week after our move, Debbie arrived to teach us how to catch the bus and how to shop at the grocery store. My friends and I followed Debbie into the store. We wandered the endless aisles and gaped at the countless brands of everything - rice, beans, milks, meats. The choices stretched infinitely before me; I didn't know where to begin. My shock soon turned to dismay. These endless stockpiles of food that surrounded me felt like a punch. How could there be shelves of food when people were starving? Just a month prior to this outing, hunger had been my constant companion. From the time I had fled my village, there was never enough food to sate my ceaseless and unabating hunger. My friends and family in Sudan still lacked food. As I stood surrounded by food that would feed the entire Kakuma refugee camp for a month, my eyes clouded over at this injustice. I lagged behind our small group, and Awino looked at me in understanding and put his hand on my shoulder. "We will have food, yes?" he spoke softly. I nodded, too overcome to reply, and we slowly walked to rejoin the others.

After a couple of weeks in America, my excitement began to wane, and I felt overwhelmed by the constant movement and the crowds always full of different strangers. Everything ran by a clock, and everything cost money. How would I keep up? My heart skipped to a race in which I didn't even know how to get to the starting line. The mass of people confounded me. I did not know how to interpret their varied expressions. And nearly everyone smiled. Debbie, her friends, bus drivers, passengers, store clerks; they all constantly smiled. I, along with my friends, spoke of this strange behavior. We decided everyone was crazy.

Confused, I finally asked Debbie, "Why does everyone smile at us? What is wrong with them?" My friends leaned forward, also eager to hear her reply.

Debbie laughed and explained, "Smiling is a show of good will, of friendliness."

"But they are not our friends," I responded. "We do not know them."

"Nathaniel," Debbie responded, "in America, people smile to say, 'hello,' or just to be nice."

I didn't quite understand, but I nodded. I wanted to fit in, so I began to smile back, but, at first, I frightened people. I would smile, and people would look at me strangely and walk away - quickly. I didn't know what I was doing wrong. When Debbie came to take us to the mall to purchase clothes in preparation for upcoming interviews, I decided to tell her of this reaction. Debbie looked at me questioningly but didn't have an answer. Still confused, I climbed into the car with Debbie and my friends and rode to a place called "the mall." We parked and walked into Belk's store to try on suits. The suits were uncomfortable and itchy, but Debbie assured us that they would help us get jobs. As we were checking out at the cash register, the cashier smiled at us, so, to show our goodwill, we smiled back. The cashier looked away quickly in alarm and barely met our eyes as we left, still smiling. When we got to Debbie's car, she burst into a fit of laughter. We didn't know why she was laughing, so we sat nervously in the car and waited until she finished.

Finally, Debbie took a deep breath before she turned to me. "Nathaniel," she began, "I believe I have an answer for you." I didn't know what she was referring to, so I waited for her to continue. "I know why people are reacting to your smiles. You can't just keep smiling. You have to be natural. You smile, but then you stop."

"I don't understand," I exclaimed.

"If you smile, you smile in greeting, and then you stop. You guys all smiled, but then you just kept smiling and staring. It's frightening people, and it makes you look crazy."

I couldn't believe it. We were trying to fit in with people we thought looked crazy, and we looked like the insane ones. Debbie saw my confusion and said, "Okay, let's practice. I will smile at you, and you smile back."

She smiled, and I smiled back. I made sure to stop smiling after a few seconds. "Okay, a little less, perhaps, but better. As I said, just be natural." Like before, I nodded, but I didn't know what natural here was. None of this was natural to me.

As we adjusted to our new surroundings, we attempted to befriend our neighbors. We were used to living in a group, so we expected to find a community with our neighbors. The majority of the people in our apartment complex were African Americans or refugees or immigrants from Iraq, Afghanistan, Bosnia, and Somalia. Sharing this bond as refugees from civil war helped us to forge some friendships, yet the stereotypes about Africa preceded our arrival and got in the way of making friendships with many of our neighbors. We were viewed and treated like the dirty ones, the criminals, the uncivilized. It was hard to convince my new neighbors that I was a human like them.

Upon our arrival, we made a point to introduce ourselves to our neighbors. They, however, made it a point to show us we were not wanted. They met our "hellos" with angry glares and would mutter under their breath to each other as we walked away; We felt alone and unsettled in this foreign land. Soon the glares became insults, and then the insults turned into overt attacks on us. One evening, we gathered at the apartment belonging to Jacob Kon, a friend, also a Lost Boy, to play dominoes and cards. As John Anyieth, another friend, was coming to join us, three African American men attacked him. They pushed him and punched him. We all rose in shock as John staggered into the apartment, his mouth bleeding. When he related what happened, we went to search for his attackers, but they, too, anticipating our reaction, had gathered their friends and ganged up on us. When the police came, our friend was still bleeding. We told them that John had been attacked, but no one was held accountable. In dismay, we asked for the police to do something to the men who attacked our friend. Rather than help us, the police instead ordered us to return to our apartments or risk going to jail.

We faced the discrimination and continued attacks from our neighbors, and on Clarkston's streets, the police picked on us. We were given police citations for little or no reason. The police would drive by us slowly if we were walking. If we were in a group on the sidewalk, we were accused of loitering and told to keep moving. Those of my friends that had licenses became used to being followed by the police. The police would often follow them for miles before finally pulling them over and issuing them a citation for minor violations that couldn't be proven in court: failure to come to a complete stop, running a red light, reckless driving, using the wrong turn signal, weaving, or crossing the yellow line.

With this discrimination from our neighbors and from the police, assimilating into our new culture was difficult. After we spent about a month in our new home, after we had some time to adapt to our new surroundings, Debbie began to speak with us about finding jobs. She began to prep us for the interviews that, we were informed, were part of the hiring process. For practice, she asked each of us a series of questions in mock-interviews: What are your skills? Why do you want to work here? Why should I hire you?

I was nervous. Everything was changing so quickly, but I was also excited. While I didn't yet understand the concept of money, I knew that it would help me succeed in America. With the UN and now the IRC controlling so much of what I do daily, I didn't feel as though I had much authority over my own life. I wanted to learn to stand on my own, to decide my own path. I had needed the help adjusting, and I was grateful for this opportunity, but I still felt lost, and I disliked being dependent on others to survive. Debbie explained that the IRC would pay our rent and provide us food stamps for a period of three months, and then it was up to us to learn to care for ourselves. I looked forward to this independence, to care for myself and my family. I also wanted to one day help others as I was being helped, so I did my best to listen to what I was being taught.

From filling out applications to the interviews, I found the hiring process difficult. I tried for more than a month to find a job on my own, but I had no experience. To confound this lack of experience, the language barrier and the etiquette of the process confused me. The interviewers couldn't understand my accent, and I couldn't understand theirs. In Dinka Bor culture, it is respectful not to look directly into the eyes of your elders or people of authority. This indirect eye contact denoted respect, as it demonstrated a recognition of authority. As this behavior had been ingrained into me since childhood, I could not look my interviewers in the eyes, so they thought I was hiding information. These painful interviews ended with the employer denying me the job; they thought I was dishonest and that communication was going to be a problem. I grew discouraged. I wanted to fulfill the promise I made to the U.S. immigration lawyer who interviewed me in the refugee camp—to come to the United States to make money to support my continued education and to find my lost family. I explained my frustration to Debbie, who reached out to the IRC.

In August of 2001, the IRC job developer, who introduced herself to me as "just Karen," brought me to interview for a janitorial position at the Georgia Institute of Technology (GA Tech). As it was a menial job that didn't require much communication, Karen helped to convince my interviewer that I was a perfect fit. As a janitor, I was to clean classrooms and offices for eight hours, five days a week. This job proved a major adjustment for me. In my community, we woke with the dawn and worked until sunset, and we worked to get the job done as a group. I never held a job before, and this sudden race against time felt unrealistic. I was either too late or too early, so my supervisor became frustrated with me. Unused to using chemicals, my supervisor taught me how to handle the various cleaners to ensure I was not poisoned. I found the concept of poison chilling, and feared making a mistake, so at first, I worked slowly and carefully, which made the workload a problem as well. Cleaning many rooms; where I walked from elevator to elevator and room to room, was tedious. After a few weeks, I adjusted to this new time-centric life. I found comfort in my new habit of going daily to a job, as I felt a renewed sense of purpose in working toward my goals, but the meager pay of eight dollars an hour was not sufficient to meet my needs. I barely earned enough money to pay my bills, and I had no idea how I was going to earn enough to make Yar my wife.

Still, even with this paltry salary, I felt hope - this position was but a step towards something larger. As an employee of GA Tech, I was eligible for free or subsidized education after ninety days. My caseworker, aware of my desire to pursue an education, informed me that GA Tech was one of the nation's top-ranking schools, and the thought of continuing my studies here, which was once not even a distant thought, thrilled me. Standing within the halls of this school kindled that burning ember within me to drink from the font of books. I especially wanted to learn how to make matters better for my family and for my home in Sudan, and with the knowledge just within reach, my fingers literally tingled with the desire to reach out and grasp this promise.

Yet, here, in this place of learning, I was confronted with a glimpse into the darker truth of many of those born into lives of privilege. As I carried out my duties of cleaning and mopping, some of the students, these best and brightest, in my presence, would callously litter the floor with their trash and create more work for me. I internalized their thoughtless actions, but, as young as they were, I took their careless disrespect as a challenge and a message that I must go to school. Their actions proved to me that book learning did not necessarily denote true education, and I also understood that through study I would continue to grow and be able to provide for my family, community, and country. So I picked up their trash and continued to work towards my goal.

However, getting my first paycheck and the subsequent paychecks overrode all of my negative feelings. It was a joyous moment to be able to have my own money—something I had never before experienced. Interestingly, with money came responsibility. Whenever I cashed my check, I paid my rent and bills and sent money to my friends back in the refugee camp. There was not enough money. I needed another check. At the recommendation of my fellow Lost Boys, I took on another job - a night job at the Atlanta Jackson Hartsfield International Airport. It was another cleaning position. My friends and I cleaned, mopped, and shampooed the airport every night.

As I adjusted to my new jobs, the conflict with my neighbors continued. My fellow Lost Boys and I worried continually about being treated equally in the workplace and in our homes. One night, thieves broke into a neighboring lady's house. In the morning, she saw my friends leaving our apartment to go to work, and believing they were the men who burgled her, she called the police. Just as my friends were about to drive out of the apartment complex, a police car pulled them to the side of the entryway. Two officers approached the car and commanded them to step out of the vehicle. Unaware of what was happening, my friends exited the car and were immediately accosted by the officers, who, without proper investigation, proceeded to accuse my friends of theft. When they began to blame my friends of breaking and entering as well as robbery, my friends, innocent of the crimes, endeavored to defend themselves. To my friends' adamant protests, the police refused to let them leave and continued to question them. Soon, the accusing neighbor and her daughter arrived at the scene. The daughter took one look at my friends and told the police that they were not the men who broke into their home. With no crime to charge them with, the police officers, without explanation or apology, curtly gave my friends permission to leave.

Frustrated with the accusations, my friends wanted to know why they had been detained without evidence for so long and, because they were now late to work, what they were going to tell their new employers. Thinking they were going to be given a notice to take to their employers, the officers instead arrested them for disorderly conduct. Even though my friends were innocent of a crime, the police brought them to jail. Panicked, I sought the help of the other Lost Boys in our community, and together, we collected the money to post bail. While the charges were later dismissed, this discrimination continued, as did the constant attacks on us. I had come to America to seek a new beginning, and I again didn't feel human. I vowed to myself that I would work harder to change my situation.

With two jobs and no car, I found myself overwhelmed. I awoke at 5:00 A.M. and my chaotic schedule would begin. I prepared for my day and rushed to catch the 6:00 A.M. bus. I arrived at GA Tech at 8:00 A.M. and, not accounting for my hour lunch break, I cleaned until 4:00 P.M. When I clocked out at 4:00 P.M., I walked to the Midtown Train Station to take a train to Five Points, where I switched trains and headed eastward to Avondale Train Station. From Avondale Train Station, I took the bus to my apartment. This trip home took two or more hours, depending on my speed of walk and the bus and train schedule. Then, I would try to find something to eat and go to sleep only to get up at 8:30 P.M. to go to my other job at 10:00 P.M. at the airport. After clocking out at the airport at 6:00 A.M., I would go straight to GA Tech to clock in at 8:00 A.M. This annoying circle became my routine for three months.

In an attempt to alleviate my exhaustion, I went to these

jobs with Yar on my mind. I was determined to spend my first dollars on getting Yar to be my wife whatever it took. I knew that these times of struggle would help me earn the privilege to be with my future wife and to bring her to America, where, together, we could work towards building education for ourselves, our family members, and our country.

One month into this chaotic schedule, I grew exhausted. I knew the importance of these jobs to Yar and me both and tried to will myself to maintain the strength to push through the curtain of fatigue, but my body succumbed to the exhaustion. At times, I would fall asleep on the train and miss getting off at GA Tech. The train would take me all the way to Sandy Springs, the last train station in the north. I would hurriedly take a train back to GA Tech and would clock in thirty minutes to an hour late. Likewise, I would also pass Avondale Train Station, my train stop to get home. My airport job was safe because my friends would wake me up, but this exhaustion began to jeopardize my job at GA Tech. My GA Tech supervisor didn't understand my situation and warned me that if I could not arrive to work on time that I would be fired. This threat terrified me, as I saw this job as the key to the education I so desperately wanted.

In this midst of this exhaustion, terrorists attacked America on September 11, 2001, killing thousands of Americans by using hijacked planes to crash into the World Trade Center, the Pentagon, and rural Pennsylvania. As I watched these burning buildings on the screen, I felt the familiar tug on the chord of terror that war had placed within me. For us, the Lost Boys of Sudan, learning that radical Islamists were behind the attack, we thought war had followed us to America. In addition to the resurgence of this familiar fear, our Clarkston neighbors targeted us. They heard that Osama Bin Laden had lived in Sudan and could not distinguish us from the Sudanese who accommodated Bin Laden.

On the night of September 11, as I was already afraid that war had followed us, our neighbors attacked us. They knew that many of us lived in one apartment, and they approached us shouting racial insults and yelling that we were responsible for the deaths of innocent Americans. We tried to explain that we were not connected to Bin Laden or his group of terrorists, but this group, blinded by their furor, continued to charge at us. I ran with my roommates and friends into our apartment while this fanatical group of citizens felt it their patriotic duty to harm us. In the attack on America, their safety had been threatened and they responded in blind, unthinking, animal rage. In this primordial mindset, they proceeded to break the window of our apartment and attempted to force their way inside. We fought to keep them outside while one of my roommates called the police. To our relief, the sound of the sirens sent our attackers running. However, as the apartment complex was large and as we had never before seen those who assaulted us so violently, there was no way to know the identity of our assailants. Without a suspect, the police were unable to bring these bigoted men to justice. They could only file a report and tell us to call if anything else happened.

In fear of further attack, the next morning we reported the situation to our volunteers who, in turn, reported the incident to the *Atlanta Journal Constitution* (*AJC*). The *AJC* wrote a piece about the attack—striking the difference between the Lost Boys of Sudan and the Sudanese government that collaborated with Osama Bin Laden.

To further this message that we were not a threat and that we belonged in our new country, our volunteers encouraged us to make efforts to show our "Americanness." We emphasized to our neighbors and colleagues that the presence of Bin Laden in Sudan contributed to our suffering as well. We bought miniature U.S. flags and demonstrated in Clarkston to express our support of America and to condemn the terrorists' actions. Knowing all too well the loss from war and out of gratitude to a nation that had opened its borders to us, we also donated money to support the families of 911 victims. As the news of our story as Lost Boys and our efforts as U.S. residents began to spread, the Clarkston community came to understand our background and a new chapter began for us - a chapter without fear of attack and the beginning of our acceptance into our community.

During this traumatic time in America, which, unfamiliar with a war on its soil, was still reeling from the shock of the attack, my own political ideology began to take form. Years prior to arriving to the United States, I could not pronounce politics, let alone participate in political issues. I was born into a country that would soon be ravaged by war. I spent my youth surrounded by this war. I moved to camps in foreign lands, forever chased by the constant reality of hunger and war. While the Sudanese Civil war was political - it was a fight for freedom from oppression and tyranny, I did not yet understand the complicated politics involved in the war nor did I understand that the freedoms for which we were fighting were inalienable human rights. Being young, I knew only the violence and the loss. I weaved through this turbulent time into my teenage years in the remote refugee camp of Kakuma, where access to social media was a luxury. I transitioned from youth to man unaware of international affairs. I had no ideology, no political identity.

In response to the Al Qaeda terrorist attacks, President George W. Bush declared war on terrorism. He responded the way I could have if I were the president. This defensive reaction mirrored the response that had been ingrained in me as a Dinka boy - to defend my home and my family against threats and attack. As a result, he became my favorite politician and a source of inspiration to me. Having been born into a family, in one of the most conservative societies in the world, the Republican ideology most closely matched my own value system. The Dinka, who believed in freedom for all, held that marriage was only holy between men and women. Homosexuality, abortion, cohabitation, divorce, and fornication, were considered criminality. Identifying with the conservative Republican principles and participating in American demonstrations gave me courage to begin to develop an ideology and a political identity. However, later, through education, my political views became less idealistic, and I adopted a moderate conservative ideology. I came to recognize the importance of a more balanced philosophy, as, from my perspective and experience, sometimes, too much of anything is a dangerous thing. At the time of the attacks, when I was at heart attracted to the Republican ideology, I was not yet an American citizen. I could not officially participate in the United States political activities.

Through these tumultuous and catastrophic events, I continued to work the impossible shifts that denied my body of the necessity of sleep. After two more tardies that I prayed would remain unnoticed, I again fell asleep on the train. I hurried to take the train from Sandy Springs to GA Tech and arrived to clock in at 8:47. My supervisor, who was waiting for me, told me not to bother clocking in and fired me.

Having lost my GA Tech job, I needed another job and found one at Bailey Street Bakery through a friend's referral. This job paid $7.50 an hour, but its schedule conflicted with my airport job. I started at 4:00 P.M. and finished at midnight and sometimes 1:00 A.M. This schedule did not allow me to go to my 10:00 P.M. job at the airport. I discussed my situation with my airport supervisor, who, thankfully, understood my predicament. She agreed that I should come in whenever I concluded my bakery shift. I managed to keep both jobs for about two months only to lose my airport job. It became difficult for me to make it to the airport whenever I was done with my bakery job, especially on days that I worked over until 1:00 A.M., when the public transportations no longer ran. As none of my Sudanese roommates had a car, I was forced to ask my coworkers at the bakery to give me a ride to the airport. Since it was late and the airport was out of the way, they were often unable, and on these occasions, I would take a taxi a distance of about 30 minutes. Paying for a taxi also became too expensive.

For a time, this problem seemed to be solved. My friend, Abraham Madit Nhiany and I had bought a 2001 Hyundai Sonata for $1000 from our friend, an African American by the name of Mario Chandler, who taught at Oglethorpe University and had become our mentor. I studied the drivers' manual and took the learner's permit test; I passed. Mario taught me how to drive in a few brief lessons. In two days, I became familiar with driving—at least comfortable enough to drive within the apartment complex. Whenever Mario left or failed to show up, I practiced alone at the apartment. This solo practice gave me a little confidence on driving.

Faced with the difficulty of coming home from work, one day I was tempted to drive my Sonata. I drove successfully to and from work. That one day of success opened a dangerous door. I began to drive illegally to work every day, with only my learner's permit. Just three nights after I began driving to work, I clocked out, started my car, and pulled onto the road. Outside of the company gate, I turned left and headed towards the light. Exhausted and anxious to get home to rest, I sped up a little as the light turned yellow. I thought the driver in front of me was going to go through the light, and I prepared to follow. He didn't. Instead, he stopped suddenly. I panicked and couldn't find the brake to stop. I hit the car hard. It was a police car. The two police officers—a captain and the officer who had been driving--quickly ran to save me. They knew I was hurt. "Sir, are you okay?" one of the officers asked. I blinked, dazed but unhurt into the searching beam of their flashlight. God had again refused to give up on me. My car was totaled, but I was fine. "I'm okay," I squeaked tentatively.

Having fully assessed that I was indeed okay, the officers resorted to their job. Their next six words sent the chill of fear through me: "Sir, step out of the car." On shaky legs, I climbed out of the wreckage that was my car. They asked if I had been drinking, to which I responded, "No." To be certain, they had me blow into a device which confirmed that I was indeed not drunk. The next question was basic: "What happened?" I lied. I told them my brakes didn't work.

They asked me for my driver's license and car insurance. I produced the insurance and the learner's permit. The first thing I heard was, "These are the kind of people we are looking for." He meant "illegal drivers." I was paralyzed. I thought I was going to jail. The two officers called more officers to the scene, and one of them proceeded to videotape the incident. Fortunately, I did not go to jail, as I surely thought I would. The officer only gave me two citations—one for the accident and one for driving with the learner's permit. The citation stated that I had to appear in court on 25th November 2001. The officer handed back my learner's permit.

The officer then asked me what I wanted to do with my car. This time I replied honestly. "I don't know." I suggested the car be towed to my work, but the officer informed me that it was private property and the company wouldn't allow it. He told me a towing company would tow the car and that I would get the information for the place. In addition, he asked me how I was going to get home; there was no public transportation that late and I had no money for a cab. Kindly, one of the officers offered to take me to the police station where they would find an officer to take me home. Without any other option, I rode in the back of the police vehicle to the police station, where, in my exhaustion, I sat napping on the seat. At 4:00 A.M., an officer gave me a ride home.

As I walked through the front door, I found all of my friends awake and wondering what had happened to me. Since I didn't have a cellphone to call and it was perhaps premature for them to report my absence to the police, they could not go to sleep out of concern for my safety. When I arrived home, out of the relieved excitement that surfaces after a fear has been proven unfounded, they all talked and laughed at once. Their excitement quickly turned to curiosity, and their laughter shifted to interrogation.

I informed them of my accident and showed them the citations. Learning that I rear-ended a police vehicle, they said I was headed to jail right after court for driving with the learner's permit. By midday, the news reached my other friends. They all were unanimously convinced I was headed to jail after court. I didn't know who told them, but I became more frightened in their certainty. This was it. I made it this far, and I was headed to jail in about a month.

Contrary to these warnings, which were accompanied by woeful shakes of the head that communicated my sure doom, our American volunteers, including Mr. Chandler, who had sold me the car, offered me encouragement. They told me that I would be fine, so long as I get my license before the court date. I made getting my license my priority. With the dangers of driving, I no longer was able to make it to my airport job, so I lost that job as well. Understanding the necessity of a car to being able to hold jobs, the Sudanese Episcopal Church of Atlanta donated one car to me and my fellow Lost Boys. Bol Maliet, who had his learner's permit and had been trained to drive by some of the volunteers, became the designated driver who helped drive us to shop, to doctor's appointments, and to work. As Bol was practicing for his road test, I asked to practice with him. He agreed, and we set up cones in the parking lot at the apartment. For two full days, we practiced.

The following week I drove with Bol and Mayom Bior, another friend, to Hapeville, by the ATL airport, for our road tests. Since we had one car, I chose to go last. My friends both failed the test, which did not help my mounting nervousness. As they had more practice than me, I had second thoughts. I felt my situation was hopeless and told them that I didn't want to take the test, that I wanted to cancel and go home to practice more. They insisted that I take the test. I did. I nervously climbed into the car when it was time, and I painstakingly went through every step asked of me. To my astonishment, not to mention relief, I passed. I proudly went home bearing the trophy of my "big license," as my friends and I called it in comparison to our learner's permits. I was extremely excited. I believed this "big license" was my only hope not to be thrown in jail, my "get out of jail free card."

On November 25th 2001, I walked shakily into court. My first time ever in court, the crowd of people surprised me. I was confused as to what I should do, so I asked the bailiff and was told to "hush" and to listen for my name. Eventually, my name was called. I was directed to stand in front of the judge and swear to tell "the truth, the whole truth and nothing but the truth." I admitted my guilt. The judge asked if I had my license, and I presented it. For a moment,

I stood crucified at the front of the courtroom as the judge reviewed my case. The choices, as told to me by my friends and volunteers, were clear in my mind—jail or freedom.

The judge cleared his throat and a cold trickle of sweat slid down my side. "Son," the judge began, "I do not believe that you acted with malicious intent or with the intent to break any laws. You have done what you could to remedy your lack of a license. You may go." As I stood blinking in sheer disbelief at the judge's pronouncement, he repeated, "You may go."

I could not believe it. In a moment of sheer beneficence, the judge dismissed my case. I had to sign some paperwork with the clerk before I could leave, but I felt elated. The vision of squandering the opportunity I had been given behind bars lifted. I guess I was still in a state of disbelief because, after signing some paperwork, I just stood in front of the clerk expectantly. The clerk also had to tell me that I could go. I nodded, still speechless, and walked out of the courthouse. I was not charged a fine nor did I have to serve jail time. I thanked God as I walked freely out of the courthouse. Once I reached the sidewalk, I burst out laughing and walked joyfully under a clear blue sky.

After leaving court, I immediately went home to inform my friends of my outcome in court. I burst through the door to find my friends sitting expectantly on the couch and around the tables. When I walked into my apartment, my friends grew quiet, their eyes wide with anticipation. I couldn't contain my wide smile, and the contagion of my relief spread through the room. My friends, anxious yet patient, listened as I recounted my day in court. Given our experience with the police, they could not believe the judge's decision either, but they, too, were relieved and overjoyed that I made it out of the court. By the end of my story, we were all talking and smiling. I looked around the room at the kind faces of my friends. I felt blessed. A bad situation worked out alright, and, more importantly, I had a group of friends who genuinely cared about my well being. That was my true gift.

Chapter Nine: An Act of Peace

While I became content in my air-conditioned apartment and no longer had to worry for food, these comforts could do nothing to assuage my fears for my friends and family. As the news trickled in through the media about the continued conflict of Sudan, we became more and more fearful. And there was also the guilt. I was given an opportunity as my loved ones and my country were still plagued by war and starvation. The constant stream of news that depicted the escalating conflict in my country added to this guilt and slowly eroded my spirit. Living so far away, I felt helpless.

One evening, as I watched the flames framing women and children fleeing frantically for their lives on a shiny, flat screen, I thought, "Yes, I'm the lucky one." I lost my family, home, country, and here I was. I worked two jobs, stridently saved every dime I had in order to marry Yar, and was no further in my education. What was I doing for my country?

I felt complacent, empty. I had to do something, so I spoke with Karen.

"What can I do here, while my family suffers there?" I asked helplessly.

"Nathaniel, you succeed by surviving and living the best life you can," Karen replied.

"That's no longer enough," I said.

We sat quietly for a while. Finally, Karen responded, "I understand." She paused briefly before continuing. "You know," she replied thoughtfully, "many people here have not heard about the Lost Boys or the war in Sudan. Perhaps you can let others here know your story."

"How?" I asked.

"You can speak at churches and schools. You can even contact your legislators, let them know that Sudan is important to the people in their district. Legislators are often unaware of what their constituents want until people start sending letters and calling them."

"How will writing and calling help?" I asked.

"Well," Karen began, "the legislators rely on the votes of the people to be reelected, so if the people let the legislators know what is important to them, and if enough people are contacting them about the same issue, the legislators realize that it is a matter that needs their attention."

I weighed Karen's words. For the first time in a long time, I did not feel helpless. I spoke with my roommates, and they, too, wanted to act, and together, we spoke to the other Lost Boys in our community. There was no need to convince anyone of the need to act. We realized that saving the lives of our family and reuniting with our long lost families lie in one achievable goal; peace. Together, we became united to achieve this goal.

We had been granted a new beginning in America, and we now saw an opportunity to speak to America about the war in our country. Our story as the Lost Boys of Sudan became the dais and the beginning of that process. For so long, even before America, I tried to shut out the memories of the nightmare that made me flee from my home and that had removed me from all that I loved. Now, it was this story that could bring peace to my land.

The first time I shared this story, I spoke before All Saints Cathedral, in Atlanta. The emotions I had long ignored resurfaced brutally and unexpectedly; I had to pause several times in the story. The resurgence of those memories made the people around me seem far away, and their voices sounded like echoes. I forced a smile and expressed my gratitude at their kindness. Afterwards, I sat in my car, overcome.

I couldn't talk to my friends, not even Yar, about how

I felt. This new pain paralyzed me, and I didn't know how to express it. Perhaps, I felt ashamed, unable to control my emotions. Still, I continued to talk, and I found with each telling, the pain started subsiding. In working to heal my country, I was also healing myself. I couldn't erase the memory, but I was the owner of my story, and it was up to me to change my story into one of hope. After all, I was here; I had survived.

Assuming the role of ambassadors and advocates for Sudan, my colleagues and I spoke publicly in churches, in schools, to our friends, and to the media. My deacon and colleague, Abraham Yel Nhial, who is currently the bishop of Aweil diocese in South Sudan, was featured in "The Lost Boys of Sudan" documentary on *60 Minutes*. The documentary made Atlanta the center of The Lost Boys story and afforded us greater access to media. *CNN*, *NBC*, *The Atlanta Journal Constitution*, and other media outlets carried the Lost Boys of Sudan story.

This interest inspired me and my friends to continue with our efforts. We saw that the people of America cared about our story and wished to make a difference. After our presentations, they embraced us and expressed their sympathies and asked how they could help. I always responded, "Please tell our story and write your congressmen." I was touched by this desire of the Americans to not be limited by borders but to care for the humanity of others, and with this extended support system, I felt a resurgence of hope for my home country.

Across the United States, my fellow Lost Boys took on the same responsibility in their respective states—bringing to light the plight of the people of Sudan and advocating our desperate quest for peace. We, the Lost Boys in Atlanta, were lucky to have the Carter Center, which provided a venue that promoted our efforts. At one point, hosted by Carter Center, we met Sadiq al Mahdi, the former prime minister of Sudan who authorized the attacks of our villages, in which we became the victims in 1987. As this man, who ended my childhood with a mere order, who had sent armies of men, pawns who blindly and obediently carried out *his* order to burn my village and kill my people, stood before me, I was shocked at how small he seemed. He was nothing but a small, wizened man. Somehow, in standing before him, I felt liberated. I didn't feel the anger I expected. Instead, I spoke to Sadiq al Mahdi, not about my loss, but about my hopes for the future. Along with my fellow Lost Boys, I instead urged him to do everything in his power to persuade the government in Khartoum to end the war. The past couldn't be undone, but the future still was yet to be written. Together, we urged al Mahdi to work for a peaceful Sudan.

On a different occasion, also organized by the Carter Center, I met Dr. John Garang De Mabior, the man who inspired me to pursue education rather than war. Because of this influence that forever changed my outlook and, therefore, my life, Dr. Garang loomed larger than life. Still continuing his efforts for a peaceful Sudan, Dr. Garang then served as the chairman of the Sudan People's Liberation Movement (SPLM) and commander-in-chief of the Sudan People's Liberation Army (SPLA). I stood in awe before him. With my fellow Lost Boys, I thanked him for the role the SPLM/A played in my life, but I strongly pleaded with him to seek peace. Together, we emphasized how the Sudanese conflict caused us loss, and that we wanted the violence to end, and he assured us that peace was his ultimate aim.

Our campaign gained momentum, and we were able to mobilize American communities and constituencies to join our efforts. We spoke, played videos, and showed statistics of Sudan's Civil War. We wrote letters to the U.S. Congress. Eventually, some of us testified before Congress. Although there were many Americans calling for peace in Sudan prior to our arrival, our efforts strengthened their advocacy.

In response to our call, many institutions and civil societies used the power of their voices and pens to push the American government to facilitate an end to the Sudan Civil War. The U.S. Christian community, the Black Caucus, and many members of Congress sympathized with our plea and made it their fight. Americans held rallies and wrote Congress on our behalf.

Fortunately, in 2002, the synergy of our relentless campaign overcame the U.S. lawmakers. Tom Tancredo, a Congressman from Colorado, sponsored the Sudan Peace Act, an Act aimed to end the Sudan Civil War. The Sudan Peace Act was officially signed into law by President George W. Bush in October 2002. During the signing, president Bush declared, "I have today signed into law H.R. 5531, the 'Sudan Peace Act.' This Act demonstrates the clear resolve of the United States to promote a lasting, just peace; human rights; and freedom from persecution for the people of Sudan. The Act is designed to help address the evils inflicted on the people of Sudan by their government—including senseless suffering, use of emergency food relief as a weapon of war, and the practice of slavery—and to press the parties, and in particular the Sudanese Government, to complete in good faith the negotiations to end the war."

Listening to these words, I felt a pride in my new nation. America, my new land, cared about me and my former home, and in my contributions, I felt a part of this change. These efforts in promoting my story and fighting for the Peace Act sowed the seeds of my interest in politics within my soul. I learned that anything could be achieved through education and effort, and I optimistically worked to educate others about my story and those who still suffered in the camps in my country. For me, this Peace Act was not an end; it was the beginning of the battle to bring adequate food, health care, and education to South Sudan.

Chapter Ten: From Refugee Camp to Hollywood

One chilly Monday afternoon in March 2002, after just nine months in the United States, I heard a knock on our door. I hurriedly jumped up from the couch, turned the lock, and opened the door. Jane Knapp, an American volunteer through the IRC, who had become our mentor and mom, beamed at us from the entryway. I eagerly welcomed her inside where all my friends greeted her with enthusiasm. As she sat down, she looked to John and said, "I have some good news, John. Dr. David Holcomb, your prosthetic specialist, received a phone call from Hollywood. They are looking for African amputees to work in *Hostile Rescue*, a movie based on the Nigerian Biafra war, starring Bruce Willis as a principle character."

"I'd be in a movie?" John replied, his eyes alight with excitement and curiosity.

"Yes," Jane, replied smiling. "If selected, you will get to be in a movie. I am here to get your picture and put together your resume," she continued.

When I heard her speak, my adrenaline spiked with excitement and disbelief. I looked from Jane to my friends who stared at her in equal mystification. We learned about movies in Kenya's Kakuma Refugee Camp, but we had never heard of Bruce Willis. In Kenya, after hard study, I used to go to the cinema to watch movies. I knew of *Commando*, an Arnold Schwarzenegger action film, *No Retreat, No Surrender*, a Van Damme's action film, and I knew most of Bruce Lee's *kung fu* films, but I had believed that the actors were fictional characters who died long ago. At first, I thought that Jane was only kidding, that John could not possibly play in a movie. Then I became afraid—I couldn't imagine John becoming a star without us. Panic set in.

"Can we be a part of the movie, too?" I blurted out, interrupting her.

Jane turned to me in surprise. "No, I don't think they will take you. You're too overweight for the movie. They are looking for skinny people for this particular film. They want refugee-looking individuals to play the role of refugees," Jane justified.

She was right. After eating for three months on IRC food stamps and then continuing to eat three times a day, a phenomenon I was still not used to, from the money we earned in our jobs, we had all put on a great deal of weight in just nine months. We no longer possessed the gaunt, skeletal appearances to which we had grown accustomed. Even according to our pre-war Dinka standards, we had become fat. However, this seemingly valid reason failed to convince me. "Can we try?" I persisted.

"Why do you want to be in a movie, Nathaniel?" Jane asked me, her voice full of curiosity and surprise.

"We want to accompany John. We don't want him to be lonely. Besides, we want to work in a movie and become stars, too," I said jokingly, yet, in my mind, I could already see myself blown up to appear larger than life on the big screen with my friends, who had become my family. I looked to them, and they all nodded unanimously in agreement.

Jane laughed and exclaimed, "Well, I can't explain in a way that will convince you." She shrugged and added, "Why not? Let's try."

As she raised her Polaroid to take our pictures, she looked into our healthy, rounded, and eager faces and shook her head. She clicked her tongue and sighed. "I want you all to put on very tight clothing to look skinny," she directed us.

"Thank you," we responded. My friends, Gabriel Magok, Awino Gam, Abraham Nhiany, Santino Garang, and I hurriedly squeezed ourselves into the clothing we arrived in, now tight and busting at the seams, while she took John's picture.

"Argh!" I grunted, struggling to zip my jeans. "This isn't working," I cried in frustration. I refused to admit defeat. All that stood between me and starring in a film was a pair of pants, and I wasn't about to allow a flimsy piece of fabric to get in the way of this new dream. I wriggled, sucked in my stomach, twisted and pulled until I victoriously fastened the clasp. I was forced to breathe in shallow gasps, and I couldn't sit down, but the jeans were on.

We walked stiffly back into the living room in our too small clothing to wait our turns. After Jane finished photographing John, she turned, took one look at our extra-straight posture, and doubled over in laughter. "Okay, okay," she said in an attempt to regain her composure. "Your turns."

Jane patiently snapped pictures of each of us and then jotted down our primary information. "Okay. I am going home to put your resumes and headshots together, and I will send them to Los Angeles," Jane promised. "It will probably take about three weeks before we hear from them." Here Jane paused. She took a breath and continued, "Look, I don't want to fill you with false hope. I know that they are interested in John; however, I don't know that they will need the rest of you, but we will make a most valiant effort. Best of luck to you all," she said. Jane turned to leave our apartment, and we accompanied her to her car like a group of impassioned school boys.

We waited anxiously for Hollywood to respond, and believing we would get to pick our own characters in the movie, we discussed our roles. Influenced by *Commando*, Schwarzenegger action film, we concluded we were going to be soldiers if accepted. After two excruciatingly long weeks, we received letters from Revolution Studios. We were all accepted to work as evacuees in *Hostile Rescue*, a title that later changed to *Tears of the Sun*. In the letter, they stated that they would soon send our airline tickets, from Atlanta to Honolulu, Hawaii, where *Hostile Rescue* was going to be shot.

In a few short days, a secretary at Revolution Studios emailed Jane our flight itinerary. Jane called us in the afternoon and told us to prepare for a ten-o'clock morning flight on the following day. Full of excitement, we hastily prepared for our departure to become big film stars. At precisely 7:30 AM on the day of our departure, Debbie Myers, our other volunteer and mentor, knocked on our door. She informed us that Jane had other obligations and that she had come to see us off instead. She said that she was in touch with our driver and that the vehicle was on its way.

We stood by the window, too excited to sit down. To our amazement, we watched elated as, fifteen minutes later, a shiny, black snake-looking vehicle, sent from ATL-Jackson International Airport, arrived at our apartment. My heart took a dive to my stomach before it surged to my throat to skip with excitement. We raced outside, gaping at the weirdest vehicle we had ever seen.

"It's a limousine," Debbie said as she stared at our amazed faces.

"A limousine, what kind of a car is this?" I queried.

"It's a luxury car used in special occasions and by special people. You are now special," Debbie cried as she hugged us. Debbie, who had assumed the role of a mother to us, was overcome by how much she was going to miss us. Her little children Chris and McKenzie held onto her arms in joy. We comforted Debbie and assured her that we would return to Atlanta. Our neighbors trickled outside to watch in disbelief. I believed that they must be curious to know why these jet-skinned individuals were entering a limousine as a white lady cried. We climbed into the limousine, which to my astonishment, was like entering a private living room full of cushioned leather seats. We expressed our astonishment as these plush seats molded to our forms. Debbie leaned in to wish us luck once more. A lump formed in my throat as I watched her retreating back as she walked with her kids to their car. We were off to ATL-Jackson International Airport. Having seen the affection between Debbie and us, the driver of the limousine asked, "Where are you from, and how are you related to that lady?"

"We are Africans from Sudan, and she is our friend," we answered.

The driver nodded. "You guys must be special. I wish you luck," he continued.

"We are not special, but thanks," I commented in response to his wish for us.

My friends and I chatted in excitement as we drove to the airport. Once there, we climbed out of the limousine and were directed to the check-in counter, where we were checked into a Delta flight destined for Los Angeles. We cleared the security checkpoint and took the underground train to Concourse E. A moment later, we boarded the plane. When everybody was seated, our plane taxied from the gate to the runway. Just as it had on my first flight out of Kenya, excitement coursed through my veins as the plane gathered speed and surged into the sky.

In about five hours, we landed at LAX, Los Angeles. We had a layover of about two hours before we boarded our final flight on Hawaiian Airlines. We soon took off, and midflight, we were given customs forms to fill out. I was puzzled. We didn't fill out any forms when we arrived in Los Angeles.

We only had to go through customs when we arrived in New York from Africa. I now thought we were entering another country. I had thought that Hawaii was a state in the United States, but I was no longer sure. I turned to my friends, and they too, didn't know anything. "Jane wouldn't let anything happen to us," I reasoned. I filled out the form as I was told.

Soon, the pilot came on over the intercom and announced, "Please fasten your seatbelts. We are preparing for landing." My heart thudded with anticipation as we began to make our descent. I felt the bump as the plane's wheels met the runway and heard the scream of the engine as it reversed to slow down our plane. Finally, we slowed to a stop. "Welcome to the Honolulu International Airport," the pilot announced. "Enjoy your stay."

As we exited the plane, a woman bedecked with flowers greeted me with an, "Aloha," and placed a flower necklace over my head. I turned to my friends in surprise and watched as they were greeted in a similar manner. Soon, we were each crowned with Hawaiian flowers.

Isabel, the casting director, and her team, along with Curtis Fuqua, the brother of the movie director, Antoine Fuqua, greeted us in the airport. Coincidentally, most people who also arrived that day were members of our group, the evacuees. At this time, we still thought we were going to be soldiers. From the airport, we drove along Ala Moana Boulevard and were checked into Ilikai Hotel, on 1777 Ala Moana Blvd, in Waikiki Beach. All of the people, except for the parents of the younger actors, who came for the movie took single hotel rooms. Still used to our communal way of life, we decided to share our rooms - two of us per room.

A bellhop led us to our room. As he opened the door, we all gasped in astonishment and slowly entered our spacious gold-bedecked room replete with plush white beds. Excitedly, I fell backwards onto the bed and was swallowed into its cloud-like softness. Reluctantly, I tore myself from the bed's embrace and walked over to my friends who stood silently in front of sliding glass doors. The memory of the beauty of the scene that greeted me still fills me with awe. I looked out the window and found myself gazing down upon a wind-rippled beach and an expanse of blue green waters. This first taste of luxury, the beauty of the setting, silenced us. We gaped for a moment at our surroundings before breaking into grins and laughter. I felt like a star.

The next morning, we were taken to the wardrobe, where a group of men, assigned to play rebels in the movie, were trying on military uniforms. We fell in love with the soldier uniforms, and as we had discussed earlier, we rushed to transform ourselves into soldiers. One of the directors stopped us. "You're not going to wear uniforms. You will be dressed in civilian clothing because you will play Nigerian refugees," she explained. We became unhappy and insisted that we wanted to play soldiers. The assistant director, who was unable to appease us, forwarded the issue to the casting and movie directors, who flatly refused our demand.

We were later called in to try on our costumes. To my dismay, I was given a unisex costume. The costume looked like a woman's shirt, and I fiercely refused it. The casting director and her team tried to convince me, but I was not ready to let anyone take my dignity away. I thought it was demeaning for a man to wear a woman's clothes, and I didn't want to be despised by anyone for abandoning my manhood. It was the worst of insults.

"I will leave the movie if you make me wear a woman's clothes," I threatened. My face flushed in anger at the thought of the embarrassment.

The casting team approached my friends and assured

them that the costume was worn by both men and women. They insisted that I wear the costume for the movie.

"Please, Chol," my friends urged. "We are doing this film together. It is not a woman's clothing. In Nigeria, it is worn by men and women."

My friends talked me into wearing the costume and, reluctantly, I agreed, so for the four months of filming, I got to wear this questionable costume. After our wardrobe fitting, we were given a preliminary orientation and then stayed in the hotel for a couple of weeks as we waited for the rest of the cast. As we basked in our life of luxury, we met more than five hundred Africans who were invited to act in the movie. Most of the members of our group were women from West Africa. After filming began, we were driven daily to the set along Kamehameha Highway, named after the Hawaiian first King, in a chartered bus. The movie was shot in the Hawaiian jungle, since it looked exactly like the African jungle. I had to shake off memories of my own journey as a child through the jungles to the safety of the camp and tell myself that I was only playing a part. After filming, our group took the bus back to our hotel. As we drove together, filmed together, and ate together daily, we quickly became a team, coworkers, and friends with our group.

Soon, my friends and I became everybody's favorite. I don't know why, but I guessed it was something about our history and our conduct. Everyone told us that we were disciplined, reserved, polite, and respectful. We befriended Antoine Fugua, the director of *Tears of the Sun*, Bruce Willis, the principal actor, the members of his navy seal team, Monica Bellucci, an Italian actress who played the American doctor in Nigeria, and almost everybody else in the movie. We worked alongside Bruce Willis and the principle cast every day in almost every scene in the movie. We appreciated our roles because not everyone got to play in every scene like us.

Every weekend, Bruce Willis invited us to either his mansion for a party or a local hall where he performed with his band, and when we were on our own, we explored Hawaii's other islands and visited historical sites in Honolulu, including Pearl Harbor, the Hawaiian kings' tombs, and the Polynesian Cultural Center. We attended Hawaiian cultural festivals and enjoyed watching the intricate hula dances.

One day, a fight broke out between my friend Awino and one of our new friends during a lunch break. In reference to our rooming situation, one of the girls called my friend Awino "gay." The real root of her anger was that Awino was not interested in any deeper kind of a friendship with her, so she accused him and, in association, us of being gay. Enraged at this harshest of insults, we encouraged Awino to fight her. Soon, we were all fighting for our honor.

The hotel manager wanted us to leave. Thankfully, the management team for *Tears of the Sun* intervened, and after a lengthy conversation, it was determined that the girl insulted us. Understanding that it was a cultural rather than a criminal matter, the management team briefed the hotel's associates about our rooming situation, and the hotel immediately gave us single rooms. I had slept in a small hut in a refugee camp with my friends and then shared a room in an apartment with them since 1988. I found that I had difficulty sleeping without them, but I also did not want to have my manhood called into question. The next morning, when I saw the dark hollows under my friends' sleep-deprived eyes, I knew mine looked the same.

As we worked at all times, night and day, with Bruce Willis and the principle cast, we were upgraded to Screen Actors Guild (SAG) roles, but we grew weary and tired from the demands of this new schedule. We felt we were not being well-compensated for this additional work, especially in light of the rumor that some of the members of our group were given pay raises. The girls of our group, who were continuously starting meetings, immediately called a meeting the Sunday after this news. As we gathered in the hotel's lobby, we learned that the agenda of the meeting was to discuss a possible strike on Monday.

One of the girls argued, "The only way we can get a pay raise is if we refuse to work." The other girls nodded and vocalized their agreement. Many "yeses" circulated the room. With no experience in such a plan, my friends and I were confused, but the girls assured us that the strike would be productive. We needed more money, so we agreed. As soon as we agreed to be a part of their plan, they turned to me. They asked me to lead the strike. My eyes widened with horror, and I swallowed back the lump that formed in my throat. They continued. They furthered that I should lead the negotiation if the management submitted to negotiation. I shook my head and gave a simple, "No, thank you," but my friends encouraged me. They said I was a strong leader and that the strike was worth it. The plan set, with me as their impromptu leader - or scapegoat ... depending on the success of the plan - we all decided to refuse to work on Monday. As a token of cooperation, we promised not to regret it if we got fired.

At dawn, our alarms sounded their shrill awakening, and we set off for the movie set. We ate breakfast as usual, but. after breakfast, when the employees from the wardrobe department told us to dress and get ready, we refused. They blinked in confusion and asked us why we refused, so I swallowed the lump in my throat and boldly and simply told them: "We want more money. We are not being paid enough for our work, so we are not working today. We would like to talk to the director and the producer."

They blinked in shock before they turned and left. Soon, the director Antoine Fuqua, the most feared person on the set, strode over to us. He was not rude, but he was tough, and no one wanted to risk upsetting him. During filming, I saw him bark his commands and watched those who didn't meet his expectations wither beneath his wrath. I thought he was a dictator but come to find out he was serious about his job. He expected quality work and no nonsense.

"Y'all want to talk to me," he said.

"Yes," I responded.

"Why don't we do it later after work, Nathaniel?" he asked.

"We are not working today, Antoine," I said, calling him by his preferred name as he had previously requested. "We want a pay raise before we do anything. We are doing more work with less pay," I continued.

"A pay raise. Even you African brothers, the Lost Boys," he said, shaking his head.

"As a team we are not satisfied with this pay," one of the ladies in my group interjected.

"No? I am trying to put some fuckin' money into your damn pockets," he cursed, "And if you don't want it, I am sending you home. You're not going to hold up my plans for today. The reason I invited you, my African brothers and sisters, to work in this movie was to give you a sense of ownership in your movie.... now take what you have or leave the hotel tonight," he threatened.

Some members of our team interjected their dissatisfaction. I intervened. "With due respect," I began, "we are working twice as hard for the same pay we started on when we worked fewer hours and had less responsibility. Others in the group have received raises, yet we receive the same pay," I reasoned, but the discussion proved fruitless. Antoine was overcome by annoyance. He said he had no choice but to send us home, and he sent for the producer, Ian Bryce. In our presence, he briefed Mr. Bryce about our demand. A quiet and patient producer, Ian asked to confirm our position, and we all said, "Yes, we are not working until we are equally rewarded."

As a compromise, he agreed to a pay raise, but we first had to work and would discuss the details later at the hotel. We refused. As a result, he called other members of management into the impromptu meeting. We were asked to again explain our situation. They told us to wait for 10 minutes while they went to confer with each other. As we waited, we promised not to give in no matter what happened, unless, of course, they agreed to pay us additional money. Ian and Antoine came back. They offered us $200 a day. We welcomed the outcome because we were paid $150 a day. $50 was more than we expected.

A few days later, some girls, who they suspected to have masterminded the plan, were sent home on separate charges. Although I lost teammates, coworkers, and friends, I appreciated their idea because it worked. We were given a pay raise as they anticipated, and I felt honored that I helped lead their initiative. From this experience, I learned that the right to collective bargaining was a part of America. Despite this brief discontent, we continue to build our relationship with the crew. We put together a soccer team, and our team played friendly matches all over Hawaii including at the Hawaiian Pacific University. The film's camera director became our team captain. I became the team midfield and forward. For the first time since we left Kakuma for the United States, I didn't feel as much of an outsider. The soccer brought back the connection I felt to my home, that feeling of flying and freedom.

As we worked closely with the cast and crew, they grew to notice our Dinka ways and began to comment on our singing. They remarked that we sang more often when we were together, at the movie set and at the hotel. Some of the workers and actors on the set began to gather around us as we sang, and people began to approach us with compliments. They said our songs were lovely. To us, singing was a part of who we were, and we were touched that others enjoyed our songs. The popularity of our singing soon reached the director, who asked us to sing for the movie. I became the lead singer and sang about eight Dinka songs to be used in the movie. Unfortunately, our songs were not used in the movie, but we were still paid six thousand dollars for singing our songs.

For four months, we enjoyed the hospitality, the warmth, and the friendliness of the Hawaiian people. We made friendships, we visited beautiful sites, and we swam in the Pacific ocean. On the last day of shooting, bystanders who came to watch on a regular basis, hugged us and asked for our autographs. A week prior to leaving Hawaii, we told our friends and volunteers in Atlanta that we wished to remain in this paradise that so closely resembled our home and where we felt we belonged. While they lobbied us to stay, a life in Hawaii was not meant to be for us.

In July 2002, we bid, "Mahalo," to our Hawaiian friends as we left for Atlanta. A month later, each of us received a check worth $4000 from Revolution Studios in acknowledgement of our roles in the Screen Actors Guild (SAG). In letters they sent along with the checks, they explained that the money was originally intended to hire more experienced Screen Actors Guild, but due to our excellent performances, they couldn't have been more pleased with our work. While the letter acknowledged our efforts, they failed to pay us what they had promised. I was stunned by this failure to keep a promise. Still, I was equally shocked that we received the check after our departure, as I believed that, in our absence, this money could have been easily pocketed, and we would have never known. In the refugee camps, this money would not have reached us, but here, in America, it was sent to us without our knowledge. I drew the conclusion that in America the rule of law is a responsibility that is indeed respected. At the time, when I had not yet witnessed dishonesty related to money in America, I believed that the fact we received the check at all was a sign of integrity and, therefore, felt compensated for my efforts.

Chapter Eleven: Possibility

Peeeeep, peeeep, peeep....helloooo! I answered a phone call one special night in 2003. "Dear brother Chol," "Is it you?" It's your brother Mathiang, said a voice belonging to my brother Samuel Mathiang Nyok.

"It is me," I replied, full of disbelief to hear from my elder brother. "How are you? Where have you been?"

Samuel and I were separated in 1984, just after the second Sudanese Civil War began and before the attacks on the village. Angered by the government's abuses of South Sudan and inspired by the rebel leaders, who had sought protection in our village, Samuel longed to join the SPLM/A rebellion; however, he developed a cough that often left him gasping for breath. Still, he wished to fight. My father advised him that he would be of no use to the rebel soldiers in a weakened state and advised him further to seek medical treatment in Khartoum and to join the SPLM/A later. My father sold two cows to pay for Samuel's journey, and Samuel boarded a ship to Khartoum, journeying into the heart of the enemy territory with the hopes of being healed.

Samuel informed me that during his recovery, the SPLA began military operations in South Sudan, capturing towns from the government in 1984 and 1985. In response to this offensive front, the Sudanese government cut off all routes to South Sudan, and Samuel was forced to remain. In the paranoia of war-time, the government began to target the South Sudanese in the North, and everyone from the South had to live in constant fear of arrest, torture, or death. Samuel, with no way to leave, decided to go to school and graduated high school in Khartoum. Shortly after his graduation, the government began to round up those from the South into a government isolated camp - he became a refugee in his own country. However, learning of his education, in 1994, the Sudanese government released Samuel from the camps and gave him the official title of "Civil Administrator" and sent him to Bor. In exchange for his freedom, Samuel received a harsher sentence. He was to convince the people of Bor, the people of his home village, to support the very government who ruthlessly destroyed their homes and families. The government in Khartoum sought to halt the movement to join the rebellion.

While Samuel abhorred his mission, he was filled with the anticipation of being reunited with our family. Unable to betray his homeland in exchange for his life, Samuel instead used his official title to provide intelligence to the SPLA and advised the youth of the community to not be swayed by the government's promises and to remain true to the South. Samuel worked to deliver news to the SPLA for over a year while he desperately sought news of our family. In 1996, he received the dreaded news. Our father was dead. This news, further fueled by a desire for reparation, and Samuel's efforts to support the SPLA increased. Soon, the government grew suspicious of Samuel's efforts and accused him of collaborating with the SPLM/A, and Samuel was called back to Khartoum, where he was imprisoned and tortured. As Samuel failed to break under torture and as the government was unable to find any hard evidence of his treachery, the government was forced to release Samuel, but he was to remain under the government's radar.

Fearing for his life, in 2000, Samuel escaped to Cairo, where he applied for asylum with the UN. Just as I had to in Kakuma Kenya, Samuel went through series of interviews and after passing the interviews, the IRC resettled him in Jersey City, New Jersey in 2004. Unused to the frigid temperatures of New Jersey, Samuel quickly sought permission to resettle in Phoenix, Arizona, where he currently resides with his wife and five daughters. We remain in constant contact to this day.

While I had been so focused on working and saving money, I had to put my own goals on hold. This call from my brother awakened my dream for education, that seed planted inside me in the Pinyudo refugee camp. Hearing how the Sudanese government still targeted and marginalized the southern regions of Sudan, I knew that it was imperative that the men and women of the South receive an education. With education, I believed we could rise above the governmental abuses, so in 2003, after learning to navigate life in America, I decided to return to school, to cultivate that seed within me. I longed to attend college, so I went to Georgia Perimeter College to learn what I needed to do. Since I couldn't present a high-school diploma, I was asked to take a TOEFL and a placement test. I passed both tests and was admitted to the college.

At the time, I was working as a cashier at Fry's Electronics. I couldn't afford to quit my job, but I desperately wanted to go to college. I immediately brought my schedule to my supervisor, who readily agreed to give me only evening hours. Excited, I threw myself full force into my school work. My professors' lessons sated a thirst that had been growing since I had been out of the classroom, and I drunk deeply from the wellspring of this new knowledge. I bathed and splashed in it, and my spirit soaked up the font. There was a new lightness in my step, and I felt the promise of the gift this learning would afford me.

After about a month into my classes, my supervisor resigned, and her replacement refused to honor the scheduling agreement. I tried to plead my situation but was told that I, too, would have to work mornings and afternoons or find another job. This demand struck me with a crushing force. While trying to make money to support myself, save enough money to bring Yar to the U.S., and trace my family in Sudan, I couldn't afford to quit my job to go to school. The reality of this situation forced me to drop out of my classes.

This decision devastated me, and I grew depressed, but I knew that I couldn't allow my mind to go down a path of negativity; I had not been down that road since the camps, and I knew that the darkness there was encompassing. I chose to focus on what I had - a safe home, friends, food, water, and, most importantly, the opportunity to improve. I knew that I was working for something greater, so I forced myself to work harder. I had saved my money from my work in *Tears of the Sun*, and with four roommates, even after I sent money to my friends and family and paid my bills, I was able to save. I decided that I would save even more. I set the goal to bring Yar to America within two years and go back to school. I had already come so far. Everything was possible.

I worked, I saved, and the doors of possibility continued to open. In January, 2005, peace came to Sudan. The government and the Sudan People's Liberation Movement/Army signed a comprehensive peace agreement. Soon after this promise of peace, the roads were opened to travel, which provided Sudanese refugees a longed for opportunity to return home. Alier Mayom, a friend and fellow Lost Boy of Sudan from my village, who didn't have an opportunity to resettle in the United States, decided to return home. Having lived in Kakuma with Alier, I knew all too well his plight; I also knew that the conditions in the villages were more impoverished than those in the camps. Everywhere in Sudan it seemed, people struggled for food and water in an endless battle just to survive. I sent him money to facilitate his trip and to provide relief to Kolmarek, his home village in Aboudit, Bor. When I last heard from my mother, she was in Kolmarek, so I also sent Alier money to take to my family along with my telephone number. Daily, I longed to be reconnected with them.

My American friends, astonished that I send money trustingly to my family and friends, often ask, "How do you know that he won't keep all of the money for himself?"

This response still shocks me. I can only shrug and respond, "He promised." Among the Dinka, a man's word is related to his worth. There isn't the question of reneging one's word. If you break your word, you lose your honor. Surprisingly, after all else had been stripped away from us, our honor was the only thing the Northern soldiers hadn't taken from us. Yet helping each other was more than about keeping our word. We grew up as each other's parent and brother. We forged a bond in our loss that no amount of time can erase; we will forever care for each other.

Alier, true to his word, delivered my message. In December, 2005, at around 1:00 A.M., I received a call from an unknown number. It was my younger brother Ayom Nyok calling from Uganda. After asking for me, Ayom claimed, "We heard about you, that you made it to America, but I needed to make sure it's indeed you."

I assured him, "I'm alive," and likewise, I whispered, "Is it you?" I had not heard news of Ayom since the attacks in 1987. Ayom informed me that he, my mother, my brother Deng, my sister Ayen, and my other brothers, Guet and Choldit, and their families were safe and in Kolmarek. Sadly, I learned that my brother Ayomdit died fighting in the war but that his wife and children were in the village. The continued war, however, still rendered the conditions in the village as dire, and he and my family were in need of food and supplies. A week later, I sent him money to take to Kolmarek to help care for our mother and family. I also sent a note that I would visit as soon as I was able. The ocean felt wide.

Chapter Twelve: Creating A Family

Four years after transitioning into my new life in America, I had saved enough money to marry Yar. Having grown accustomed to our small snippets of conversation, I was nervous to reconnect. I feared that Yar would find me too changed from my new life. I wondered if she would still want me. On a conscious level, I knew that these thoughts reflected my fear, and I pushed them forcefully out of my mind. I reminded myself how easy it was to speak to Yar through our many conversations since I left. When I spoke to Yar on the phone, her voice came to me across the miles and erased the vast ocean between us. Rather than having a relationship that relied on a physical presence, these conversations enabled us to build a friendship that spanned time and place.

I visited the INS to begin the procedure to bring Yar to the United States. I had no idea how technical the process was just to marry and bring my wife home with me to Atlanta. I first had to marry Yar, and then I had to return to the states and complete an I-130 application form and other documents that supported our relationship. Following the completion of these steps, and granted that our application was approved, the approval form would be mailed, along with a money order for $420 to the Visa Center in New Hampshire and then to Kenya, where Yar, who would be waiting for the opportunity to join me, would be interviewed. I blinked at the complexity of the process and walked out of the office, discouraged by the numerous steps but encouraged that the process was begun.

Now that I knew these details, I began to fulfill the expectations of me for Yar's dowry. As a Dinka woman of a notable family, I had to honor her worth. For more than five years, I shared a three-bedroom apartment with five other friends, so only paid $400 a month in rent, I saved my money from working in the movie, plus I had held two jobs throughout my first year in Atlanta, GA, and I made sure to save everything to fulfill my vow to Yar. Proudly, I sent $15,000 to my brothers to purchase forty cows that were to be delivered to Yar's father and relatives in her village Werkok. In addition to the cows, I sent $5, 000 to Yar's paternal Uncle John Wuoi in Kakuma. As soon as I received news that these gifts were received graciously by Yar's family, I immediately purchased a ticket to Kenya. Three years, 40 cows, and $5,000 later, I returned to Kakuma refugee camp to marry Yar.

As I boarded my flight to Uganda, I was giddy with anticipation. Throughout the entire eighteen-hour flight, I found myself unable to close my eyes. My mind, too full, flew with the plane across the wide expanse of blue. As The Ethiopian Airline bound for Africa, I couldn't help but recall my flight to America; when I left full of visions of a new life. It felt strange to be headed back to the camp. I felt a mix of excitement, hope and guilt; I had begun a new life, while so many of my friends and family still suffered. I flew from Atlanta to D.C. to Ethiopia and finally, Entebbe, Uganda. Only able to focus on reconnecting with Yar, the entire journey passed in a blur, and by the time I landed in Uganda, I was jittery from the heady blend of a lack of sleep and excitement.

Once in Uganda, I took a bus from Kampala to Nairobi and then boarded another bus to Kakuma. I squeezed into a seat with a man who was also headed back to the Refugee camp. Hearing the Dinka dialect used as the native tongue sent a surge of longing through my soul. I loved my new land; however, my heart never truly left my homeland.

As we entered Kakuma, my heart plummeted as I found the wasteland of the camp unchanged. I stood in horror at the edge of the camp as I had as a boy thirteen years ago. Skeletons of animals, scattered on top of a ground of a red and dry dusty earth, encircled the camp in vacant welcome. No life grew here. The verse, "For you are dust, and to dust you shall return," sprang unbidden into my mind. I pushed the thought away, but it lingered, a sour, foul-smelling ghost.

I walked through the gates into Kakuma and felt the desperation and hopelessness pressing in on me from all sides. I swallowed, choking down a lump of heaviness, and continued to walk in search of Yar.

Soon, I heard a familiar voice cry out, first in question, then in exclamation, "Ability? Ability!" I turned and was met by the beaming face of my nephew Reech Mayen.

Taken back by the hopeful expression upon his thin, emaciated face, I had to pause a moment before I clasped his arm and said, "Hello, Reech. It's been a long time."

Reech, untouched by the melancholy that crept into my spirit at seeing my friend, my family, my people sustained by the fine thread that just kept them alive, clasped my arm and excitedly exclaimed, "How is America?"

America to those I left behind glittered like a vivid dream, both distant and untouchable, just beyond words and reach. I smiled and said, "Everything is busy, and everyone is fat."

Reech smiled at this and patted my stomach in good humor. "Come on, my brother. Let's prepare for you to meet Yar."

As we walked, Reech told me of the camp. Nothing had changed. Rations were doled out sparingly to the ever-increasing body of people that sought a place of refuge from the ever-raging war machine that was unsparingly fueled by the oil, minerals, and blood of my people. Guilt pierced my heart that I had been given a future while my people suffered under the greed of a power-hungry government that did not recognize the humanity of my people, Sudan's native tribes. While my family and Sudan were always close to my heart, like many people who are far removed from suffering, there were days when my own personal sufferings; would I be able to pay rent, would I make it to work on time, what would I eat for dinner, made these other sufferings; will I have shelter, will I eat today, will I see my family again, will I live, seem distant and removed. Maybe I had become an American after all.

As I walked through this camp that was once my home, the full weight of the blessing that my opportunity to go to America had bestowed upon me became clear. While I felt lucky when I was first chosen for America and I wanted to make a difference to my country, I felt an intensified sense of responsibility to Reech, to my family, to those who remained behind. While this surge of renewed duty coursed through me, the thought of marrying Yar lifted some of this weight. I imagined us as a united team, working together to make Sudan better for our families and future generations.

I returned with Reech and was welcomed by my friends and cousins, who already hearing of my arrival had begun to prepare the wedding luncheon. This luncheon, which, in accordance with tradition, was held one week before the wedding was where I would first see Yar. My heart leapt in anticipation. My friends and family would prepare the food for my side, while her friends and family would prepare the food for her side.

Finally, the preparations were complete, and I walked with my Uncle Reech Kuol Reech and my cousin Reech to the tent they had erected to house the guests. Soon, Yar's family arrived with Yar, and I finally had my first sight of Yar, who was talking and laughing happily with her cousins and friends. I stood speechless, frozen, unable to move. Blood rushed to my face as Yar, who realized that my capacity of movement - and speech - had momentarily abandoned me, walked over to me. She lowered her eyes shyly and said, "Hello, Nathaniel."

"Hello, Yar," I simply replied, cursing myself for the words, which had become my companion before my arrival here, flew again just beyond my reach.

We stood before each other, silent and unsure, and the doubting, negative voice began to tug at my mind. Did she still choose me? Just as soon as this thought entered my mind, Yar shyly lifted her eyes to mine before she smiled and quickly looked away. In that fleeting moment when our eyes met, I knew. She was still my true partner and love.

While many people were at the lunch, we managed to go for a walk, where we talked about our upcoming union.

At first I didn't know what to say, so I said, "I am so happy to see you," and immediately felt embarrassed by the silliness of this comment.

Yar, who seemed to sense my discomfort said, "Nathaniel, I never doubted that you would come for me. You are a man of your word. Now that you are here, you have proven the seriousness of your love and intentions to marry me as your wife."

These words, which flowed from a place of deep understanding reaffirmed to me our connection. "I know nothing of love, Yar, but I promise to do my best to be worthy of you," I responded, touched by her perceptive kindness.

"I, too, know nothing of love, but I care for you, and I see your honor. You are my family and I can learn to love you," Yar replied.

I nodded my agreement, and these simple and honest words served as our prenuptial agreement. In a traditional

Dinka world, our marriage would had been prearranged or approved by our parents, relatives, and community, but since we were both lost children without parents in the refugee camp, we followed our hearts. We promised to spend the rest of our married life in getting to know, love, and live a happy life. We knew we were created for each other, and we knew others would soon see our love.

Later, I learned that Yar's apprehension about my safety as an African in America never truly dissipated but grew the longer I was away. My return assuaged her fears and reaffirmed my commitment to her.

The next week sped by in a blur of preparation. As Yar and I both did not have our immediate families present, both of our extended families prepared for the feast for our respective sides. And, as Yar's cousins were helping Yar with the elements of the wedding thankfully beyond me; the dress, ceremony, and music, I rarely saw her.

A week after my arrival, I finally entered the ceremonial tent, a makeshift structure of poles and blankets, to sit before the pastor. My groomsmen walked me to my seat while Yar's bridesmaids walked her to her seat, and we sat side by side. My groomsmen, family, and friends sat on my side, forming a half-circle, while Yar's bridesmaids, family, and friends formed a half-circle on her side, and together, both sides formed a complete circle, symbolizing that both Yar and I, as well as our families and subtribes, were joining together as one. As I sat in this circle, my heart swelled with pride that Yar would soon be my wife.

Guests who knew us, stood in a circle around our two sides, while others from our community, and those who happened to hear that there was a wedding, gathered just outside of the tent. Weddings, which were followed by celebratory dancing, provided a light within the monotonous days of the camp, where food, life, and comings and goings were monitored closely. If someone knew of a wedding close to them, they went to participate in the festivities.

After everyone was seated, both sides began the ceremony. On Yar's behalf, her Uncle John Wuoi spoke first and emphasized how a daughter was to be treated.

"Yar is our daughter. She is to be treated with respect and dignity. She is to be cared for, even when times are hard. You will now be her husband and friend and father, so it is up to you to care for her like a daughter."

Another elder on Yar's side continued, "Now that you are married, you will give up some of the things you want at the expense of your relationship. You must relinquish previous companies and companions as a respect for each other."

My uncle spoke on my behalf: "It is important to try to talk out your disagreements. Avoid help from others who tell you to give up. You are entering into a sacred union, and in doing so, you will be father and mother to each other."

After both sides gave their advice, the pastor offered a prayer on our behalf. Yar's uncle and my uncle then took Yar's and my hands and joined them together in show that we were now united as husband and wife.

Everyone rejoiced, and we then left to feast and dance. That is all I remember of that night: the fact that Yar and I were finally one and our dancing well into the night. After the wedding party came to an end, Yar, whose friends remained with her for the full week before the ceremony, bade her friends and family a final farewell and returned to my area of the camp with me as my wife and companion.

Yar and I remained for two weeks in the camp before Yar accompanied me to Nairobi, where I would catch my flight back to America and where Yar, who would stay with her maternal uncle Dengtiel Ayun, would remain until I could arrange the paperwork for her to join me. It was still too dangerous for Yar, a woman, to return to her family in Sudan, as her village was still subject to attack, and, sadly, the barbarians heading these attacks brutally captured and raped the Dinka women, the cruelest tool of genocide and war.

My three weeks with Yar after our wedding did not feel like enough time, and soon, I was again bidding Yar goodbye, this time as her husband. Immediately upon my return, I submitted the fees and filed the paperwork to enable Yar to join me in Atlanta, and after a year of grueling paperwork and interviews, Yar joined me in America.

I left the realm of my friends and moved into a two bedroom apartment with Yar. Having Yar with me in our new home proved to me that love lifts, love believes, love hopes, and love endures. On our first night together, Yar and I vowed to never overlook this fact, for we were the only inspiration for us. Through the years of waiting, we were both more than aware of how life is attached to marriage. She was a part of me through happiness and struggle, even when we were continents away. As I embraced this beautiful woman - my wife, mother, father, brother, sister, friend - I proudly addressed her by her Dinka nickname: "Man e Nyok" (Mother of Nyok), a reference to our future son.

Chapter Thirteen: Fields of Green

Whenever my friends and I were not consumed with work, we spoke of the soccer we played in Kakuma. What remained unspoken was our fear of memory, our longing for our family, the loss of our homes in Sudan. In these conversations, I felt and heard a longing that existed in the camps, a longing, persistent and encompassing, that still haunted me. While our situations were improved, our new lives in this new land did not erase our war-torn past. It didn't remedy the fact that we were struggling to adapt in a land as foreign to us as we were to it. In these stories, I heard voices longing to be raised up. I realized my friends needed a strong bond that once saved us in the refugee camp, to enable us assimilate into our new land. I, too, felt this need and founded the Lost Boys soccer team.

This emptiness born of loss haunted all of us; mine threatened to consume me and Yar both, and she encouraged me to build the team. "Nathaniel," she advised, "I need you to be happy. Build your team, for you and for us."

I recruited all the boys who I played with in Kenya. As my motley team of refugees formed, other Sudanese boys who came to the U.S. from Egypt became interested and also joined us. We had the team. Now we just needed a space to play. In my search for a soccer field, I discovered Armistead Field in Milam Park, and, as it was in the middle of Clarkston, it seemed the perfect spot. The field, a large rectangle carpeted with green grass, sat at the base of a hill that offered an excellent view to spectators. Tall pines surrounded the field and added to the feeling of being removed from the hustle of the city. As I walked towards the field, I noticed a sign affixed to the chain-link fence that framed the field. The sign stated that anyone who wanted to use the field must get permission from the City Hall. To me, with the old rusty baseball nets standing forlornly at either end of the field, the field looked deserted. With the field obviously not in use, I didn't think that we would have difficulty receiving permission. I felt dismay that we had to receive permission to play in a public park; however, I knew all too well the dangers in not following specified procedure. I was determined to use the field and immediately called City Hall and was told I needed to obtain permission from Coach Cooper, the former Little League coach responsible for scheduling the fields of Milam Park. I called Coach Cooper, who immediately gave us permission to use the field.

I, along with my friends, played soccer every weekend. Just as it had in the camps, the soccer served as an escape. As we battled on the field, we forgot our problems and just focused on the game. Other refugees joined us in droves. Playing with teams of eleven players, we still had about four teams waiting on the edge of the field to take a turn. To ensure everyone had a chance to play, we set minutes for the game. If there wasn't a winning team, we tossed a coin and the winner of the coin-toss played the next team. These afternoons refreshed our spirits and completely changed our outlook about our birth-homes, the war, and our new home, and in our escape, we reconnected with hope.

We played without incident for three weeks. Yar commented on the impact these games had upon my spirit; she said I seemed lighter. I saw this same lightness reflected in the faces of my friends. These weekends gave us something to look forward to again.

On the fourth weekend, we met as usual. We divided into teams and began to play, losing ourselves in the freedom of the game. About thirty minutes into the first game, the Clarkston police arrived and ordered us to stop. When we asked why, they just demanded that we leave at once.

One of the teammates stepped forward, hands outstretched, and asked, "Why are you asking us to leave? This is a public field."

"We had a call about a disturbance. You have to leave," the officer replied.

Fearful of angering the authorities, we reluctantly dispersed. We were confused. We had permission, so we weren't breaking any laws. We weren't loud or drinking or causing a disturbance. I thought that perhaps I misunderstood Coach Cooper and that I was supposed to call each week. We left, and when I returned home, I called him. He was confused.

"No," he replied. "There should be no problem. No one is using the field."

Believing that we met the city's obligations of permission, we met again the following weekend. Again, the police showed up and told us to leave.

Confused, I stepped forward. "Why are we being told to leave? We aren't breaking any laws. We called the city and have the permission of Coach Cooper."

"We don't have to give you a reason. We are telling you to leave."

Again, we left. Again, I called Coach Cooper and received his affirmative response that we indeed had permission to use the field. "No one uses the field any longer. You guys are the only ones who are requesting its use, so I don't understand the issue."

I followed up the phone call and went to the City Hall and requested to speak with Mayor Swaney, whose secretary informed me I needed an appointment. Frustrated at this point, I explained that I needed to speak to Mayor Swaney as soon as possible and explained the situation. After giving me an appraising look, she reluctantly went into Mayor

Swaney's office, returned, and informed me in an irritated voice that he would see me.

I walked through her office and into Mayor Swaney's office. "May I help you?" asked Mayor Swaney as I entered the room.

I took a breath to calm my nerves, as I knew my agitation would not help the situation, and then I explained the hassle we were being given over the use of the field. I asked him why we were being kept from playing on a public field after having been given permission to play there.

After a momentary pause, Mayor Swaney responded, "I am not aware there has been an issue. You will need to contact Coach Cooper. He is in charge of scheduling Armistead Field."

"I have done that," I replied. "Twice now."

"Perhaps try him again. Maybe there was an error in scheduling," Mayor Swaney suggested and then looked at his door, which I took as a sign that our conversation was over. Confused, I walked out of his office. I don't know what I had expected; a phone call to clarify the situation, a more affirmative declaration of permission from the town's authority figure, but I did not expect to be dismissed and told to do what I had already done.

While the situation had me frustrated, I was not ready to give up. Soccer provided healing to us, and I was determined to be able to play. Per Mayor Swaney's instructions, I called Coach Cooper, who expressed his surprise at our difficulty. I asked him if he knew of any issue with our playing, and Coach Cooper, likewise, had not received any instruction that we could not play there. He told me that we had his permission.

Believing I had righted the situation, we again met the following Saturday. Again, the police showed up. Again, they demanded for us to leave. I felt as though we were running in circles. While I desperately needed the game, I didn't want to let down the team I had built. I called the City, Coach Cooper, and tried again - and again. My friends and I came to the conclusion that we weren't being allowed to play because we were foreigners. This awareness struck me in a dark place deep inside of me I did not know had existed. I see it now as a loss of innocence. While we had been harassed by the police for minor infractions in the past, I told myself we just needed to learn the ways of our new land. Now, after being turned away from playing a harmless game on an abandoned field in a public park, I felt like a foreigner in a place I was doing my best to make home. The message I heard was "You are not welcome here."

I stepped forward in an attempt to reason with the officer. "I don't understand the problem," I stated. "We were told to get permission, and we did that. Coach Cooper gave us permission to play here."

"Well, we are here to tell you to leave," the officer responded abrasively. His partner and the four officers from the other two cars stepped forward, widening their stance and placing a hand on their belt in warning.

"But we have permission to be here. I even went to the Mayor, who … " I began, but the officer took another step forward and, interrupting me, replied, "You boys need to leave, or you will be under arrest."

"But Coach Cooper …" I began, only to be cut off once more.

"This isn't Africa, where you don't follow the law. Here, we have rules," the officer stated, his voice dripping with contempt.

"We followed the rules," I began. "We have permission …"

Again the officer interrupted me. He did not want to hear what I had to say. He was there to make me leave. He made that fact abundantly clear. And, as no one seemed to know anything, everyone was able to keep us running in circles. "I am not going to repeat myself, son," the officer snarled at me. "Leave now, or you will be arrested."

Confronted with such injustice, I didn't know what to say. We followed the rules. We had permission. But we were outsiders. Worse, we were African. The officer's refusal to listen coupled with his racial comment confirmed my suspicion. And I, well, as a foreigner, I had no recourse.

Soccer was important to me. It had given me hope during the greatest trial of my life, and I needed a glimmer of that light now. We all did. We continued to show up to the field, and we continued to be told to "get lost."

Having fled from marginalization and facing continued discrimination in my new home, I again chose to go back to school. I saw education as the only way to raise myself out of the inferior labels that kept being placed upon me. In June 2005, after Sudan's Peace Agreement, with Yar's encouragement, I again decided that it was time to go back to college. Since I was out of school for a while, I had to first obtain a GED. I took the GED and passed all of the tests, but, economically, college still wasn't feasible. I no longer had four roommates helping with rent - it was just Yar and myself.

I continued to send money to help my family and friends in South Sudan, and after seeing the deplorable situation in the camps and knowing that education was the key to rise out of the ashes of that existence, Yar and I decided to send a few of our younger relatives to receive an education in Kenya, whose schools far surpassed the quality of those in the camps. While we couldn't send everyone we wished to help, which, truly, would be every child, we were able to provide scholarships to my nephews Reech Ayom and Matiop Ayom and Yar's sister Agou Mayom. Yar and I both wished to bring education into Sudan, but the education of girls, whose worth depended upon the dowry she could earn her family, was especially dear to Yar, who longed for that opportunity for herself. In South Sudan, girls were taught to care for their homes and husbands, so it was difficult for families to see that their daughters, too, could bring about positive change to the country. With these obligations, our own desires for education were placed on hold. Again, I waited.

As I continued working menial jobs to support my family, I felt in my heart that school would lead me to something greater, that I had survived and came to the U.S. for a reason. Yet, while my situation was by far greater than it had been in the camps, I felt helpless against the walls constructed of a man-made monetary system that determined my worth. So I worked, and I prayed.

While, as one man, I lacked the power to create a just world overnight, I chose to fight a battle that I believed I could overcome. I crusaded against the injustice I immediately faced over the fields. I continued to show up, and I continued to be sent away.

After a couple months of this battle just to play on an abandoned and public field, I contacted the volunteers and friends who welcomed us to America. Appalled, they contacted the Atlanta Journal Constitution, who immediately wrote, "Refugees Find Hostility and Hope on Soccer Field," that brought the injustice to public attention.

In the article, Mayor Swaney declared that the park was used strictly for baseball. Yet the Little League team that last used it had disbanded a couple of years ago. Mayor Swaney then put forth the "lawn" argument. After all, we "big guys" might harm the grass.

I was excited to see an article published that would bring awareness to the public about our struggle to play a mere game on a public - and, moreover, an abandoned - field. Yet, as I read the article, my hands shook violently. I placed them flat upon the table, yet still, they shook. Mayor Swaney's comments confirmed what I feared most: the refugees were not welcome. I was not welcome.

The awareness hit me with the force of a blow, and I staggered beneath its weight. It slowly dawned on me that the laws in America were far from black and white. If they were, I would have been protected. I followed the posted rules and expected steps, yet these actions were not enough. Underneath these surface and written laws lay a darker truth, an ugly reality. These laws meant nothing. One of the volunteers I spoke with used the line, "Smoke and mirrors." These laws were a mask, a pretense used to protect the town from those individuals deemed lesser in the eyes of the socially acceptable society - American born and white. And after everything I had been through, the triviality of it all - the pointed, extravagant effort to ban people from playing a mere game while so many people struggled for food, shelter, their lives - seemed absurd.

While Mayor Swaney, cowed by the backlash of this article, granted a youth refugee team called The Fugees access to Armistead field, my friends and I never received permission to play. We had been told to "get lost," and these words remained, immovable and fixed. While these words didn't destroy us - we continued to rise in the morning, go to work, and walk among the people of Clarkston, they allowed us to see the invisible wall that loomed between us, the field, and our town. But now that I had stood before this invisible wall, I couldn't unsee it - it loomed large and dark.

PART THREE: THE RETURN

"The usual hero adventure begins with someone from which something has been taken, or who feels like something is lacking from the normal experience available or permitted to the members of society. The person then takes off on a series of adventures beyond the ordinary, either to recover what has been lost or to discover some life-giving elixir. It's usually a cycle, a coming and a returning."

~ Joseph Campbell

Chapter Fourteen: Crossing the Threshhold

Throughout my education, I have been impressed by the healing power of words. Former Uruguayan President Jose Mujica's stated that, "Those who consider me poor fail to understand the meaning of wealth. I'm not the poorest president. The poorest is the one who needs a lot to live. My lifestyle is a consequence of my wounds. I'm the son of my history. There have been years when I would have been happy just to have a mattress." This statement strikes a chord that reverberated through my whole being. I am a Dinka, a member of the most isolated society, in terms of modernity, in the world. Although poor, my family didn't look for wealth beyond our compound. Our lives, my life, were the capital they needed.

I believe Sudan's civil war has devastated my community, and far worse, my country; lives, tradition, and culture were brutally uprooted in the names of religion, power, economics and modernity. Yet I am struck by how this devastating conflict has availed me an opportunity I could not have gotten in life without my wounds. The conflict placed me in refugee camps in Ethiopia and Kenya and, as a result, introduced me to education, which began under a tree in Pinyudo when I was nine years old, with one-third of an exercise book, a pencil, and, when there was no pencil, my fingers, which drew the numbers and letters in the dirt on the ground. For generations, and historically, even before Sudan was established as a country, my family has lived as farmers and pastoralists. Modern education, in terms of school or modern infrastructure, was never a part of the livelihood in my community's life. Growing up, I knew family, community, cattle. I do not say this to show that I ended up on the wrong side of the world but to emphasize that I was born into a marginalized and exploited society.

I realized that if I didn't make the leap and begin school, I would remain marginalized in my new society. There would always be some reason to postpone my dream. In January 2007, I made the leap and became a full-time student at Georgia Perimeter College. Interested in pursuing a degree that would enable me to be of help to Sudan, I chose to major in International Affairs. Yar, aware of the new financial burden my return to school placed upon us, took on extra hours in her job in the J.C. Penney's warehouse. At Perimeter, I took the core classes that would enable me to then pursue my major.

Entering into the realm of education was like entering a new and promising world. I suddenly found myself surrounded by like-minded people who sought to both learn and make a difference in their worlds. In my English composition course, my instructor, Dr. Ramming assigned the class a personal essay topic, "How did you end up in this class?" In my essay, I wrote on my journey to the United States, my goals for education, and about my dream to build a school in South Sudan. Dr. Ramming, compelled by my story, invited me to remain after class to further discuss my goals. She then invited Yar and me both to dinner at her home to continue our discussion. Full of compassion and a desire to help us bring our dream to fruition, she encouraged Yar and me to establish a non-profit organization; she even went so far as to provide me with a link on establishing a non-profit organization. Dr. Ramming went beyond her duties as a professor; she opened her home and her heart and offered guidance applicable to what I wanted to do with my life. I immediately poured over the information provided in the site. Suddenly, a dream that had so far been an idea began to take form.

I learned I needed a name for my organization, a mission statement, a direct goal, and a tax identification that officially established my non-profit status. Yar and I chose "Ambassadors for Change," in reference to the title "ambassadors" my fellow Lost Boys established for ourselves in our efforts toward the Sudan Peace Treaty, as the name for our nonprofit and decided that together we would continue to serve as ambassadors for South Sudan and establish much needed education in our home. As our purpose, we decided that we would build a school in Bor, Jonglei State, my home and an area central to the tribes in that area. I recalled how the UN desecrated us in Pinyudo, and, in doing so, I learned to view all of the Lost Boys, not just those of my tribe, as my brothers, and I believe that if the children of the different tribes learned together that they, too, could become united and tribal warfare would cease. For our mission statement, as we aimed to educate both the boys and girls of the nearby tribes, we decided it should be "to provide accessible education to the citizens of South Sudan regardless of race, gender, religion, or cultural belief." I applied for a non-profit tax identification, and in February of 2008, Ambassadors for Change was born.

I continued to focus on my courses, but I was excited to have established a formulated organization that would serve to make a school in my village a reality. With a new fervor, I threw myself into my studies, and in January 2010, I transferred to Kennesaw State University. I continued to speak to my classmates about Ambassadors for Change, and Audrey Ruark, inspired by my story, brought it to Dr. Hoerrner, a Communications professor who was actively involved in human rights issues at Kennesaw University. Dr. Hoerrner immediately became an advocate for Ambassadors for Change and encouraged me to speak to my professors about my goals.

Following her instruction, I asked Dr. Collins, my professor in Introduction to International Relations, if he would allow me to present my story and my organization to the class. He agreed, and I shared my story. Dr. Collins, like Dr. Hoerrner, offered to support my efforts. Learning a great deal from Dr. Hoerrner's and Dr. Collins's advice, I asked them both if they would be willing to be a part of the board of directors for Ambassadors for Change. They both agreed and quickly became invaluable sources of advice in growing my organization while I was at Kennesaw and after graduation.

While still at Kennesaw, Dr. Collins informed me of an internship opportunity with Senator Johnny Isakson's office and encouraged me to apply. I immediately went to the Student Career Center and learned that Senator Isakson accepted applications every summer, and recognizing the value of this opportunity, I applied. I secured an internship and worked with Senator Isakson from June through August 2010. As a legislative intern, I had an opportunity to meet formidable U.S. policymakers and foreign dignitaries. I attended significant meetings, hearings, and briefings with personalities like Madeline Albright, John Kerry, Hillary Clinton, Henry Kissinger, and other notable lawmakers.

The timing of my internship, the peak of the Southern Sudan referendum, did not escape me. As an intern, I was able to partake in the decision making that was the outcome of a war that had forever shaped my life. In that moment, in that time, I was where I wanted to be. A ranking member of Foreign Relations Subcommittee on African Affairs, Senator Isakson brought me along to all meetings concerning Africa. While I learned a great deal in all of the meetings, it was my meeting with Thabo Mbeki, the former South African president and chair of the African Union High Level Implementation Panel that truly developed my political skills. President Mbeki led a delegation of four distinguishable Africans, Pierre Buyoya, former Burundian President, Abdulsalami Abubakar, former Nigerian President, Thabu Mbeki, former South African President, and Amina Mohamed, African Union Representative to the United States, who, in response to the Sudanese government's request that Southern Sudan referendum be postponed, came to advocate for the Southern Sudan referendum with the United States Congress.

Our meetings with this delegation made my heart pound with anticipation and anger. Angry that after all of the fighting, the North still wished to oppress the people of South Sudan, my people. I sat at the edge of my seat and wanted to shout, "Of course South Sudan should be free! We have been marginalized and abused by the North for decades, and we must have our own voice in order to fight for our rights as human beings!" Instead, Senator Isakson calmly acknowledged the political difficulties associated with passing the referendum and adamantly agreed that the referendum couldn't be delayed for a second, that it must be held on time. He suggested that we establish timelines as we worked to garner the support of both Congressmen and South Sudanese.

After I quelled the embers of my own passion, I added my own voice to the planning process. I echoed Senator Isakson's statements and stressed to the delegation that we couldn't, as South Sudanese, afford not to vote on January 1, 2011. Our shot at freedom, which so many paid the price for, through blood or loss childhood, was finally within our reach. The U.S. Congress supported our argument and the Southern Sudan referendum was held on time. Had the U.S. accepted the postponement, there couldn't have been the Republic of South Sudan. I feel honored to have been a part in making the referendum a reality. To me, this delegation allowed me to use the life I had been gifted to make a difference for my country.

I also felt immense gratitude for President George W. Bush, who ardently supported the South Sudan referendum. While still at the Senate, I chose to write President Bush so that I could personally thank him. I wrote:

Honorable President George W. Bush,

My name is Nathaniel Nyok. I'm originally from Southern Sudan and currently an American citizen majoring in International Affairs with concentration in diplomacy and international service at Kennesaw State University in Atlanta, Georgia. I came to the United States of America in 2001 as one of the group known as the lost boys of Sudan.

I have dearly desired for quite too long to put credit where it belongs by thanking you for being the United States greatest president ever, and for your leading role in the freedom of the people of Sudan, but just could not do it due to the lack of connection. Fortunately, in the first session of this summer, I had a blessed privilege to intern for Senator Johnny Isakson (R-GA) and I was able to get your current contact.

Mr. President, the people of Sudan have endured marginalization, torture, rape, death, slavery, lack of human rights, and so forth in the hands of Islamic governments in Khartoum, but finally they are free because of your exceptional and strong leadership. I have never missed any of your speeches and I remember you saying, "freedom is a God's gift to all mankind" regardless of their identity. I believe this ideology drives your decisions and you have greatly inspired me socially and politically.

On behalf of the people of Sudan, although not authorized, I personally thank you for your contribution to Sudan peace and freedom even though you were burdened fighting Islamic extremists and strengthening America at every capacity. Few individuals could do what you have done. All Sudanese were hopeless about the future of Sudan, but at your watch, the United States of America midwifed the Comprehensive Peace Agreement between the Sudan People's Liberation Movement and the National Congress Party. This peace agreement brought an end to the civil war that has wrecked the Sudan for more than five decades and the people of Sudan are now enjoying the peace dividends. Last April, the people of Southern Sudan, who have not participated in elections since Sudan's independence in 1956, concluded nation-wide elections at all levels of government. Although, they were not fair and free according to international standard, the elections instill hope in me that Sudan would one day become a democratic State. On January 9, 2011, the people of Southern Sudan will hold a referendum election to decide their fate as an independent Southern Sudan State or a United Sudan second-class citizen. As they wait for the referendum day with joy and excitement, they have you in mind. You deserve thanks and we, the people of Sudan, owe everything to you and I give you credit for whatever the future of Southern Sudan will be.

As a Southern Sudanese, I believe you have blessed the people of Southern Sudan with the opportunity to enjoy their God given freedoms, and I hope the fight for democracy is on. As an American, I thank you for protecting America, strengthening our country at all fronts, and spreading democratic ideals so that freedom reaches those who have been denied human rights for years. You're a phenomenon—and I regret not being able to vote for you because I became an

American citizen in May 2007. I wish there was a third term for you, but your conviction, firm leadership, and great accomplishments made you a champion. I pray that you live the longest and may God strengthen you with wisdom and knowledge and bless you forever. Please relay my regards to Mrs. Laura Bush, the twins, and your parents.

Sincerely,
Nathaniel Chol Nyok

In response to this letter, President Bush sent me the below hand-written note.

Dear Nathaniel,
Thank you for your very touching letter. I appreciate your kind words.
I hope you are doing well. Laura and I are doing great here in Texas.

Best regards,
George

While the letter was succinct, I felt honored that President Bush received my note and touched that he took the time to acknowledge me. I was only in school and was already able to begin to participate in change for both of my homes. This reality that my voice mattered filled me with a hope and strength I had been reaching for. Everything seemed possible.

Chapter Fifteen: Family Reunion

In January 2009, after 22 years of separation, I traveled to South Sudan to be reunited with my family. I felt overwhelmed. I couldn't believe I would be reunited with family lost to me for years. Yar was excited to meet her mother-in-law and brothers-in-law. Meeting my family, she said, was a special gift. Eagerly and with trepidation, we began to prepare. Yar and I purchased gifts of clothes, blankets, mosquito nets and shoes to give to my family and friends in the village.

My brothers Chol Nyok and Deng Nyok met my wife and me in Juba, the capital of South Sudan. They could not believe it was me. The years had turned my younger brothers into grown men, and we had to convince each other of our relation. In my mind, my brothers remained frozen in the last memory I had of them , as young boys. My brothers, now men, were strangers to me. They smiled and talked, and my heart swelled with pride that these men were my family and would be back in my life.

In Juba, my brothers introduced me to people from my community, who had a delegation that was going to my village for a conference. As the road was not safe, my brothers and I were told to travel with them. We drove to our village, where I was reunited with my mother, whose voice and songs remained with me throughout my journey. Meeting my mother was very emotional and was not what I had expected, and yet it was more. I arrived to my village with the delegation. My mother, who had heard the news that I was to arrive at any hour, then waited, as I entered the village, she hurriedly ran to meet me and the delegation. She hugged Yar and me. Rather than a private meeting, we met in public under a shady tree which served as a conference hall that day.

The passage of time made me unrecognizable to my

mother. I had to reintroduce myself to my own mother. It was a strange feeling. After I assured my mother that it was indeed me, her own Chol, my mother cried and sang in praise of God for me. I felt overwhelmed but held back my tears. My mother's emotion shocked me. We were not alone. Emotional displays were not a part of my culture, and while I was overcome with emotion, I did not know how to react. This woman, my mother, touched my heart. She reached out to touch my cheek, and I was home.

My mother and family impressively welcomed my wife into our family. I thought my mother would have some reservations since she didn't contribute in the choosing of my wife. Given my situation, she completely understood the reason I didn't wait for her approval, and, more significantly, she highly praised my wife. Her acceptance of Yar lifted the fear of rejection from my shoulders; my new family and my childhood family were now one.

After a great deal of tears and hugs, my mother walked me through the death of my father. Ever since my mother's letter in 1998, my father's death had been a huge question for me. I knew he died in the early 90s, but how? Sickness? War? Sadly, having grown up in lands ravaged by war, these deaths were the only deaths I knew. Finally, through my mother, I was able to learn my father's story. Through more tears, my mother informed me that my father died when Dr. Riek Machar, the former South Sudan vice president, who turned rebel against SPLM/A, invaded my village in 1991. He died defending the village. Learning the truth of my father's death struck me as though he had just died. The absence of my father, my inspiration, felt like a sharp, physical wound. I comforted myself with the belief that my father was an angel interceding to God on my behalf. In my mind, he was still the figure who would watch over me, my guardian angel who would protect me and keep me safe. Yet I missed him.

Two days later, my mother celebrated my return by hosting an official welcoming ceremony. Everybody in the community was invited. Although the shadow of my father's loss hovered over me, I enjoyed the ceremony. The community prayed for me—elders sprinkled my wife and me with water as my mother cried over me. Although I didn't ask for my share and waste it on foolish living, my mother picked the gospel of Luke 15:32, which reads, "It was meet that we should make merry, and be glad: for this thy brother was dead, and is alive again; and was lost, and is found." The connotation of those words, her choice, spoke to me. To them, I was lost and dead, but now I was found alive. Found. The word hung in the air and I welcomed it into my heart.

The depth of my mother's love, boundless and enduring, inspired me. In college, I had conversations with fellow American students about family. I learned phrases like, "I hate my father or mother," and "My parents didn't want me. I came by accident." The narrowness of these responses angered me on a deep level, as I would give anything to have grown up surrounded by my parents, my family. Sometimes, I couldn't help but to respond, "In the world of technology, your parents could have dealt with that accident by another accident. The fact that you're alive means they love you and want you to succeed in life." This intrinsic response to such statements became even more true when I reunited with my mother. After our years of separation, she treated me as special; I could feel the depth of her parental love. There is nothing like parental love, which is unlimited and timeless, a true blessing without a substitution.

As I participated in the village gatherings, I was comforted to see the values and customs that I knew as a child were not lost. I was also excited to see schools under trees. I asked my mother about these schools.

"I had not heard of school until I was in Pinyudo. What are these schools here?"

My mother responded, "Many of the teachers were lost like you. They returned to teach us of the life beyond our village. They tell us that to survive, we need to learn, so parents want their children to learn. As doctors, lawyers, and leaders, they can help us."

Emotion swelled in my heart. Parents were willing to send children to school, and children sat under the trees, wide-eyed and eager to learn. I identified with these children because I, too, began my studies under a tree. I knew all too well what it was like not to attend a class because of the weather conditions. Seeing this new value for education in my community awakened my purpose. I felt that education had saved me for a reason, and I had been wanting to make a difference in my home, to make my survival, my life, matter. I decided then and there that I would work to build a school in my community.

In less than two months, I had to return to the United States. My mother wanted me to stay longer, but I convinced her that I had to finish my studies so that I could better help her and those in our home. I promised to visit with her regularly, yet, as I bid my mother a tearful goodbye, I knew that the visits would not occur as often as I would like.

As the plane took off to take me to my home in the states, a new sense of elation overtook my being. I finally felt liberated from the fear of not knowing that had engulfed me for years. As the plane rose above the clouds and into the infinite blue of the sky, I felt invigorated with a renewed sense of purpose.

Chapter Sixteen: South Sudan's Independence Day

The referendum for South Sudan's independence was to be held all over the world on January 9, 2011. In October 2010, a group of Lost Boys and I formed South Sudan for Freedom, an organization aimed at informing our community about the importance of voting for separation. We worked diligently to convey the importance of the freedom of South Sudan to many of the South Sudanese who, having witnessed the destruction of our homeland and foreseeing the struggles in becoming a new country, feared the ramifications of separation. I served as the Secretary General and a spokesman for the organization and worked to rally the South Sudanese to vote for the separation. I reached out to Lost Boys in other states and planned and led meetings, where my friends and I stressed the importance of South Sudan becoming its own country. As an independent nation, we would no longer be marginalized by the North; we would have a voice over our land, and most importantly, over ourselves.

These meetings were a success. Now, after having gained immense South Sudanese support, South Sudan for Freedom wished to enable these South Sudanese a voice in this momentous occasion. Through personal donations, the support of the IRC, and our church, we arranged for twenty vans to carry us up to Nashville's Tennessee Center from Atlanta, GA. Our efforts coupled with the implications of the vote received media attention, and two CNN journalists rode with us to document this occasion. I rode to Nashville, excited and full of anticipation, in one of those vans. When we arrived at the voting center, we gaped in wonder at the numerous South Sudanese who spilled out of the Tennessee Center to form lines that wrapped in promise around the building. These South Sudanese had journeyed from Mississippi, Kentucky, Tennessee, Florida, and North Carolina--whose residents had a choice between voting in Tennessee and Washington, D.C. I was elated at the turnout. These other Lost Boys were also still fighting for our country, and their joy was palpable.

I stood in one of these lines that curled around the outside of the building of the Tennessee Center. The steady drizzle of rain gleamed off of the sidewalks and slowly seeped through my clothing and skin, yet I stood lead-singing, talking, and cheering in the extensive line with the other South Sudanese--I didn't feel the rain. Instead, I felt the surge of excitement, the hope. I watched in amazement as a lady tore her Sudanese passport into pieces as she shouted, "Bye-bye, Old Sudan, slavery, and Al Bashir!" Another man sang the biblical verse asserted by Moses during the Jewish struggle, "Let my people go." Soon, everyone in the lines picked up this verse, singing these words of freedom while waiting to vote: "Let my people go----let my people go----let my people..."

As I happily waited, the words of the song that I sang as I fled for my life from South Sudan to Ethiopia repeated themselves in my mind: "Na pïïr raan ku rum pinyde, ke bï ŋuëën ŋö. Cakkë thäär abï naŋ adhëŋ töŋ döŋ. Kɔ̈th ke baai, Thudän panda. Acuk bï com në kë peei, Aaye wɔ nyïn wɔ jeny mɛn thäär.--" A person without land is lifeless. Let the war rage on. There will be a survivor, a seed of the nation. Our Sudan will never be sown with different seeds, but us, the liberators." Soon we would have a land. We were the survivors. We were the seeds of hope, and we were voting for the future of our country. I realized at that moment that the dream of my people, the dream for freedom, depended on my vote, on all of our votes--our votes were the votes of redemption.

A total of 902 people turned out at the Nashville Center for this historical event, and on February 7, 2011 the longed-for results were announced: 98.8% of the voters had voted for separation. Of this near unanimous number, only four people voted for unity in our Nashville's center. A small number of South Sudanese still remained confused; they remained divided between voting for unity and separation because at the time, South Sudan interim government faced uncountable challenges in becoming a new country. In terms of infrastructure, South Sudan currently had nothing; no hospitals, no schools, no stability, yet it brimmed with hope, for the seeds of this New Sudan would strive for the success of our country, and I longed to take part in the birth of my country.

Soon after this momentous vote, I received an invitation from the Ministry of Foreign Affairs. Dr. Akec, a South Sudanese who served as Sudan's Ambassador to Washington, D.C. during the Comprehensive Peace Agreement, who was now about to become the first South Sudanese Ambassador to Washington, D.C., had been impressed by my contributions in our secession campaigns in D.C. and with my efforts in South Sudan for Freedom. He made sure that I received an invitation from the ministry to be present as an honorary guest for South Sudan during its first Independence Day. Excitement coursed through me at this invitation. This ceremony would serve as South Sudan's declaration of independence as a new country to its people and to the world, and I, Nathaniel Nyok, had been invited to take part in this marker in my country's history.

I immediately contacted airlines to try to obtain flight tickets. The price of the tickets was staggering. I called every airline that flew into South Sudan and then any country around South Sudan that would enable me to travel safely into South Sudan; Kenya, Egypt, Ethiopia. Thoroughly disheartened, I hung up the phone. The impediment of the expense rendered my invitation useless. Money, in itself, papery thin and meaningless, stacked itself into an insurmountable wall, one that blocked me, after all of the fighting and the loss, from partaking in the freedom of my people and the birth of a new beginning. I immediately went to Dr. Hoerrner and expressed my frustration.

"I am so sorry, Nathaniel," Dr. Hoerrner responded compassionately. "I know what an opportunity that trip would have been for you."

Disheartened but grateful to Dr. Hoerrner for listening, I left her office. Again, money loomed, encasing me in its tall, inward-leaning walls.

One week after this discussion, Dr. Hoerrner summoned me to her office. I arrived at her office to find Dr. Prochaska, a business professor at Kennesaw, standing next to Dr. Hoerrner. Both professors beamed with uncontainable excitement.

"Nathaniel," Dr. Hoerrner said, "I would like to introduce you to Dr. Prochaska who was deeply moved by your story."

"Hello, Nathaniel," Dr. Prochaska began, kindness filling her voice and eyes. "Dr. Hoerrner told me about your background and your organization as well as your recent invitation to be an honored guest at Sudan's Independence Day. I wanted to do something to help, so I held a fundraiser. An anonymous donor has contributed an amount that should cover your expenses to return home and perhaps purchase the land for your school."

Unable to speak, I stood there completely mute, my mouth forming to say something, but I couldn't form a coherent thought to even begin to express my gratitude to these women. Dr. Prochaska extended her hand, offering me an envelope. Silently I took this generous offering of hope from her outstretched hand, and tears rushed to my eyes. Embarrassed, I managed a quiet, "thank you," unable to speak more in light of the tears that threatened to overwhelm me. I nodded my appreciation.

As I walked home to Yar, I was overcome. With no one to see, I tilted my face towards the sky and allowed my tears to wash over my face. All of my dreams were becoming a reality; I am married to a beautiful, supportive woman who was also my best friend; I was working towards achieving my education; I officially founded an organization to build a school in my home village; I was able to return to South Sudan to witness its birth as a new nation after so much bloodshed; and now, with the purchase of the land, my organization was more than a sheet of paper with a goal; it was becoming a reality. I would be a part of changing the future of my people. In the past, I suffered the rains of a fiery war, yet I now stood beneath the rains of blessing. Dr. Prochaska didn't understand that she gifted me a greater gift than a plane ticket or land. While I struggled daily to make my survival meaningful, to somehow give meaning to the screams and sufferings I could never forget, I was finally able to make my survival matter. Dr. Prochaska handed me my life.

Before my departure, I had to complete my courses. Filled with hopes of a new dawn for my country, I completed my final exams on May 9, 2011. I had earned 18 credit hours and made the Dean's list, and, especially as I was about to embark on a journey to witness my home reborn as an independent, sovereign nation, I recalled Garang's words on the importance of education: "You, the youth, are the 'seeds of our nation." We count on you to become doctors, engineers, politicians, diplomats, pilots, and leaders of all kinds for New Sudan." I felt pride in my accomplishments and in my country, being one of many seeds of hope for South Sudan realizing my goal of education, and was going to be there for the birth of my homeland as an independent country.

On May 10, 2011 I boarded a plane at ATL Jackson International Airport via Amsterdam for South Sudan. After a brief stop in Nairobi, Kenya, I finally arrived in Juba, South Sudan. The mood in South Sudan pulsed with excitement and anticipation. The South Sudanese had begun celebrations for their New Country two months prior to the actual Declaration Day, and my own heartbeat quickened as my eyes burned with proud, joyful tears.

I reported myself to the then Ministry of Regional Cooperation which later became the Ministry of Foreign Affairs and International Cooperation. Aware of my South Sudanese background and contributions to the independence efforts, the Ministry officially invited me as a guest to the Declaration of Independence. A lump formed in my throat as I readily accepted this honor.

On July 9, 2011 at 6AM, I arrived at the Dr. John Garang De Mabior Mausoleum, and I was seated with great privilege. I sat merely inches away from Susan Rice, the United States permanent representative to the United Nations and the head of President Barack Obama's presidential delegation to the Republic of South Sudan, which includes Colin Powell, former secretary of state and chairman of joint chief of staff; Barrie Walkley, United States Consul General in Juba, South Sudan and Donald Payne, Ranking Member of House Foreign Affairs Committee on Africa, Global Health, and Human Rights. Also in attendance were Johnnie Carson, Assistant Secretary of State for the Bureau of African Affairs; Carter Ham, Commander of the United States

Africa Command; Brook Anderson, Deputy National Security Adviser, Chief of Staff, and Counselor for the National Security Staff; Donald Steinberg, Deputy Administrator for USAID; and Ken Hackett, President of Catholic Relief Services. This collection of notable USA delegates was but one of the several distinguished delegations that came to witness the Declaration of South Sudan's Independence.

My badge, marked USA guest, indicated that I was an American but held a birthright and special blood connection to South Sudan. Pride filled me, as I was invited to sit with these remarkable individuals as a result of my daily efforts in the United States for my country. Being able to sit in the midst of foreign dignitaries including many presidents was a blessing. As tears swelled over my eyes, I watched the flag of old Sudan being lowered, signifying the end of its brutality and dominance over my people. In incredulity, I celebrated the flag of the New Sudan, now The Republic of South Sudan being raised, highly exalted, adjacent to the flag of the United States of America. The sight of South Sudan's flag, colored black for land and identity, white for peace, red for blood in defense of South Sudan's sovereignty, green for plentiful natural resources, a blue triangle for the blessing of Nile Waters, and a yellow star for the unity of South Sudanese diversity, awakened me to the realization that I was truly experiencing the dawn of my country.

I witnessed the arrival of the numerous South Sudanese and the other invitees. I watched foreign officials as they paid respect to Dr. John Garang. I saw the crowd sing, cheer, cry, and scream. Many fell due to hot weather, excitement, and fatigue. I gazed in awe at Pagan Amum, Secretary of the Sudan People's Liberation Movement as he drummed up the crowd, leading them in a cheer for South Sudan; at Agau Jongkuch Nhial, Secretary of Government of South Sudan, as he invited speakers to the podium; at James Wani Igga, the Speaker of South Sudan's Legislatively Assembly, as he read the Declaration of Independence's Proclamation; at Salva Kiir, South Sudan's President, as he gave his reception speech; and at Omer Al Bashir, North Sudan's President, as he gave his conceding speech. I repetitively wept for joy. I knew something huge had happened. Millions of South Sudanese shouted in elation and waved the flag of the Republic of South Sudan excitedly in the air.

At that moment, I realized that I had contributed to something significant—the independence of South Sudan, the land that had consumed millions of lives. Our people sacrificed lives and blood to lay a foundation for our country. They have passed the baton to us, "The Founding Generation". My heart surged with loyalty.

As Susan Rice walked up to the stage, I recalled her strong stand for the South Sudanese and peace throughout North and South Sudan. I recalled President George W. Bush's decisive leadership that led to the signing of the Comprehensive Peace Agreement (CPA) between the Sudanese government under the National Congress Party (NCP) and the Sudan People's Liberation Movement (SPLM). I recalled President Barack Obama's courage and soft foreign policy that deterred Sudan from violating the CPA, which led to the referendum where the South Sudanese voted overwhelmingly for Separation. I recalled the devotion of the Black Caucus and how hard it had lobbied for peace in Sudan. I recalled Condoleezza Rice's hard work and dedication to our cause. I recalled Tennessee Senator Bill Frist's special contributions to Sudan Peace, his friendship with Dr. Garang, and his support of the South Sudanese. I recalled Missouri Senator John Danforth's tough diplomacy that kept the Sudan Peace negotiations and continuity of Sudanese dialogue despite the difficulty. I recalled the Sudan Peace Act in 2002, brought about by a bill sponsored by Congressman Tom Tancredo of Colorado, which was passed by the United States Congress. I recalled the former Secretary of State, Colin Powell signing the CPA on behalf of the United States in Nairobi, Kenya. I recalled Senator John Kerry and Secretary of State Hillary Clinton's trip to South Sudan in support of South Sudanese Peace during the referendum. I recalled my colleagues, the Lost Boys of Sudan, as we campaigned in the United States for peace in Sudan. I recalled the letters and messages of the American people to the United States Congress on behalf of the Sudanese. I recalled the American churches that campaigned for peaceful Sudan. I recalled Senator Johnny Isakson of Georgia and me sitting in his office with Thabo Mbeki, former South African President and head of the African Union High Level Implementation Panel(AUHIP) and his colleagues, Pierre Buyoya, former Burundian President, and Abdulsalami Abubakar, former Nigerian President, as we discussed the significance of holding the South Sudanese referendum as scheduled, and I recalled Jimmy Carter, through the Jimmy Carter Center, as his team monitored the Sudan election and the South Sudanese referendum election.

My heart throbbed with expectation as I waited for Susan Rice to speak. Finally, she spoke: "On behalf of President Obama, the United States delegation, and the American people, congratulations on your independence." The crowd roared its approval before she continued, "My government, the United States of America, will stand with you all the way." With her last remarks, my excitement boiled over. I stood and cried, "USA! USA! USA! USA!" The Sudanese crowd, foreign Presidents, Premiers, Kings, Queens, Princes and Princesses, Ambassadors, and Government officials, some of which are unfriendly to America, gaped at me, thunderstruck. I noticed that all eyes were on me, but I didn't care; my exhilaration poured forth not only from my body but from my soul and spirit. Perhaps it is my own optimism and enthusiasm, but as the dignitaries continued to watch me, I optimistically believed they noticed my Sudanese appearance and "USA Guest" badge, and I believed they realized that I had every reason to shout "USA" at the heart of this momentous occasion for South Sudan. By dusk, I was exhausted, but there was no better reward than nationhood. Five days later, the United Nations welcomed the Republic of South Sudan into the world community.

With the independence of South Sudan in July 2011, I became a full person and no longer a refugee, no longer a wanderer, no longer homeless, and no longer a lost boy of Sudan. I officially became a true citizen of the world and of two sovereign nations—the United States of America and the Republic of South Sudan. Interestingly, both nations celebrate their Independence Day just five days apart, and I'm privileged and blessed with the opportunity to get to celebrate two Independence Days every July. However, the fight for democracy and prosperity continues not only in South Sudan but within my heart.

The day after the Independence Day Celebrations, I traveled to Bor with the sole purpose of being a part of this fight. I wanted to arm my people with the pen of knowledge, to help them ride the winds of victory to understanding and peace. Upon my arrival in Bor, I set an appointment with Governor kuol Manyang of Jonglei State. Due to the festivities, the Governor Manyang was unable to meet me until the following week. As with all dreams, I wanted to see mine come to fruition at that moment; however, time had taught me that patience and faith brought great reward. So I waited, and in one week's time, I arrived at the Governor's office and eagerly waited my appointment.

Soon after my arrival, Governor Manyang walked out of his office and approached me. "I hear you have a proposal that I will want to hear," he stated, shaking my hand. I explained to Governor Manyang that I believed that my school in Bor, which would stand central to the tribes, would help eradicate tribalistic wars and facilitate peace, improve lives by promoting skill sets that would generate income, and foster a sense of nationalism, which would be integral as South Sudan establishes its identity as the world's newest country.

The governor openly declared his support of my efforts. He provided me a letter with his signature that promised the land to my school and directed me to meet with Commissioner Maker Lual Kuol of Bor County, who redirected me to the Civil Administrator Mabil Duot, who finalized the deal. I paid Mabil Duot for the land, and, after consulting with the committee, he promised to allocate the land to my school.

I left Duot's office with my letter of promise. South Sudan had been born. I had survived war and loss and was alive to help raise my country in its new beginning. "Dad," I whispered out loud, "I wish you could see this."

Chapter Seventeen: The End and the Beginning

When two years after I graduated I couldn't find a job, I became frustrated. The majority of jobs in International Relations required a Master's degree, so without much choice, I decided to go to graduate school. As a prerequisite for enrollment in graduate school, I had to first pass another test - the GRE. So much of my life changes depended upon a test, and again I was nervous. I took the GRE and scored 139 out of 170 in verbal reasoning, 143 out of 170 in quantitative reasoning, and 3.5 out of 6 in analytical writing. I passed.

After taking GRE, I contacted The George Washington University, Catholic University, Georgetown University, Fletcher school at Tufts University, and School of Diplomacy and International Relations at Seton Hall University. I was daunted by the amount of tuition these programs cost, but I knew my continued schooling was necessary for my success. Without a parental support or a scholarship, I chose Seton Hall because it was less expensive in comparison to the rest and it held the major I chose to pursue; M.A. in Diplomacy and International Relations. Making education a priority, I convinced my wife to quit her $15/hour job to move to New Jersey. Fearful of leaving a home in which she had just learned to feel secure was frightening to her, but she supported my decision and stated, "In order to succeed, we must first sacrifice."

We moved from the moderate winter of Atlanta to the frigid cold of New Jersey in December 2013. Unfamiliar with the northeastern extreme of cold, Yar and I shivered in layers of clothing in a hotel room in this new home. Upon our second day here, I left our cubicle of warmth to sort out my classes and find a place for Yar and I to live. I arrived excitedly to the campus to learn that my loan was not sufficient to cover the tuition of $1100 per credit, and I needed 45 credits for my program. My average tuition every semester stood at about $15,000, which did not include books and other educational requirements. As a full-time graduate student, I couldn't apply to a full-time job, but I couldn't secure a part time position either. I faced the threat of a hold on my account at Seton, which would not allow me to register for the classes that began in January unless I pay the entire amount. I felt the angry stab of panic. In response, the doubtful part within me chastised, "I just moved Yar and myself away from our friends and home for nothing." This could not be the case. I wouldn't allow it. As our savings quickly dwindled paying for a hotel room and the snow raged to a mean fifteen inches around us, I pushed back this negative voice, and I looked to find a way.

I returned to the apartment to find Yar distraught. War broke out once more in South Sudan, this time between the Dinka and the Nuer. Our families would need our support more than ever. I had no idea how I was going to do this when I couldn't even find a way to take care of Yar and I. Now, more than ever, I could not give up. My family and my country needed me to succeed.

In order to afford an apartment and pay for tuition, I was forced to obtain a loan. This idea of borrowing made me feel indebted more than just financially. I felt as though I had lost control over my own life, and I did not like that feeling. I reminded myself that this small backwards step would result in numerous steps forward in the end. With the loan, Yar and I had just enough to rent a small studio apartment for $850, and I used the rest of the money to pay for my tuition.

Now, I was officially enrolled in my classes, but I didn't have the money to purchase books. Once classes began, I explained my situation to my classmates, who kindly allowed me to borrow their books. I was embarrassed to ask for their help, but I knew if I allowed pride to rule me that I would not achieve my goal of attaining my Master's.

While I had taken care of the immediate concern of my education, finding a way to pay rent and other utilities in New Jersey became a constant pressure. My wife, who had transferred her job with J.C. Penney from Atlanta to New Jersey, suffered a pay decrease from $15 to $11 an hour. Not only that, her hours also decreased from 40 hours a week to barely 20. Each month, Yar and I struggled to pay our rent. My best friend, who also doubles as my maternal distant cousin, Jacob Kon had a car that's registered with UBER in Washington, D.C. I pleaded with him to let me drive with him. He accepted my request, and I traveled to Washington, DC every weekend to drive for three days in downtown D.C., which, while it brought in an additional $250 a week, it was exhausting and a burden on my studies.

Barely able to meet our own needs, we still had our own families in Africa who needed our support. Knowing the value of family and community, this responsibility became a constant source of strain. We could not disconnect from our families in Africa. Their lives depended on us. Supporting our families was one of the reasons I sacrificed to further my education. We continued to send money to our two families and relatives in South Sudan and to my nephew, who I sponsored to go to school in Kenya. Juggling bills, school, and family throughout the duration of my grad school took a mental and physical toll. For two years, our lives became a dreadful hell.

As part of my degree requirements, I had to fulfill a ten-week internship. In the Spring of 2014, I interned with Save the Children in D.C. to complete this requirement. In about a week, my co-interns—Ameerah, an American with

Afghan background, Pema, an American with Chinese background, and Moria, Sarah, and Jeff, all natural born Americans, became my friends. Ameerah, Moria, Pema, Sarah, and I worked in a small office, which, in reference to our seriousness, Kari Reid, our manager nicknamed Sirius. Jeff, who worked in an adjacent office, visited with us every day.

Even with all of our seriousness, Sirius - and Jeff- became a family. Ameerah even became my Arabic teacher, teaching me Arabic alphabet and sound. We began to lunch together every day. New York Deli Market on 20th and L streets soon became our favorite lunchtime haunt, our Sirius turf, especially on warm days when we dined outside. Every work day in a team spirit, we hugged, we chatted, we consulted, and we joked. With this uplifting company and the impact we were making, work was fun.

One day, Moria, Sarah, Jeff and I went for lunch at our favorite place. While lunching, Moria quietly left. She came back with twelve lit cupcakes. As she approached, Sarah and Jeff looked at her with eager smiles. As I turned to see the reason for their smiles, Moria started singing, "Happy Birthday to You." Sarah, Jeff, and everybody at the New York Deli Market joined in singing, "Happy Birthday to You, Dear Nathaniel." It was a surprise birthday celebration for me—the first ever celebration of my life. At 35 years old, I felt like a newborn baby. I never knew this beautiful group of people, who solely by profession became part of my life, would break my family's long tradition of not celebrating birthdays. To me, it was a special moment.

After an extended applause, I remained fixated to my chair, perplexed and dripping with sweat. I didn't fully understand the situation, and my adrenaline rose in response to my confusion. Then came a weird moment. As I searched to find the words that would express the thankfulness I felt in my heart, Moria seemed to interpret my response and stated, "Nathaniel, make a wish and blow out all the candles."

"Ah," I responded.

"Make a wish and blow out all the twelve candles," Sarah supported.

I couldn't understand the tradition. I simply sat there, unschooled in the ritual of birthdays.

Sarah noticed. "What do you want to have in life?" she asked.

"I wish for many things," I replied, unsure how to select one thing.

"Okay, close your eyes and make a wish; then blow out all the candles," Sarah said.

I closed my eyes and said, "I want a good life."

"No! No! No! You can't tell us. It's a secret wish," they all said. "Just make a wish in your heart and blow out the candles."

I closed my eyes again, and then I blew out the first candle.

"Blow them all out at once," they said.

I blew out all the candles at once. They all cheered, and I felt educated, and, in a way, brand new.

As my new work was bringing me joy, war raged on in South Sudan, and Save the Children sent my colleague Sonia Khush to assess the groundwork in the displacement camps. She immediately came to me and asked where my family was located, and I learned she was going to the location to which my family had been displaced - Awerial County in Lake State. Tears filled my eyes. Every day I worried and longed for my family. The fact that I worked for an organization who sent people to the area where my family took refuge reinforced to me that I was pursuing the right path. Soon I would be the one to go and help my family. Sonia kindly took down my mother's name, and I put her in touch with my brother Deng Nyok, who was to meet her in Juba and help her get in touch with my mother.

For two weeks, I waited, anxious to hear news of my family. Finally, while I sat at my desk at Save the Children, my telephone rang. I answered, expecting the call to be work related. Instead, it was Sonia. Her voice full of excitement, she exclaimed, "Hi, Nathaniel. I have someone here who would like to talk to you."

I couldn't speak. My hands began to shake as I held the phone more tightly to my ear. I fought back tears when I heard my mother's voice. "Nathaniel, is it you?"

"Yes, Mama, it is me."

With that, my mother began to sing, her Dinka words taking me back to the time when she would wrap me in her arms and my world was still safe. "Nathaniel, do you remember?"

I did not remember, yet I remembered the feeling, safe and warm.

"Nathaniel, that was your song, your childhood song."

I wanted to ask her to sing it again, so I could hold onto the words, but she had to go.

"I love you my son. You have made me proud."

I was once told that being a survivor is a feat, but that label is limiting in its own right. It's not enough to survive. To truly live, to thrive again, one must first heal, to find the promise in each new day. My mother's voice washed over me, reminding me of that promise.

Shortly after I returned to New Jersey and my studies at Seton Hall, I received a call from Meghan Higginbotham, a staff member of the Enough Project, founded by human rights activist John Prendergast. John Prendergast would be attending the screening of *The Good Lie*, a film that featured the assimilation of three Lost Boys into their new home in Kansas. John Prendergrast invited me to speak at this event. Excited to help raise awareness, I eagerly accepted.

On October 8, I journeyed to Kean University, where I received a warm welcome from John Prendergast and the members of Kean's Human Rights Institute. I walked onto the stage and into a glare of lights and applause. It always impresses me how the lights create the feeling of standing alone before a crowd of people. I shared my story. I told about my home, my hundred-day march to the refugee camp, my journey to America, and my dream to build a school. Telling my story is always both painful and cathartic, and I was grateful for the audience's supporting applause when I had finished.

After the event, Jeffrey Toney, provost at Kean and writer at *Huffington Post* approached me. He was moved by my story and offered to help raise awareness for my organization and to support the cause in any way he could. Touched by his sincerity and compassion, I accepted his offer with gratitude. With each new friend's support, I have felt a renewal of hope. My mother had taught me that I would have many guides along my path, and it was my job to be open to their lessons, and throughout my journey, I have indeed been blessed to have had many guides.

One year later, when I finally walked to the stage to receive my graduate diploma, both of my parents were with me. I could feel my father's pride, hear my mother's song. After the ceremony, Yar embraced me, and I knew - "this is just the beginning."

Everything I went through, every place I have been, every person I have met has led me to where I am at in this moment. While at times I struggle with the sword of memory, I work to let that memory propel me forward, not backwards.

I have let go of the anger. As I work to build a school in my home village, I am filled with hope for tomorrow. I believe education can save the young boys and girls of South Sudan, just as it had saved me.

My identity has brought me unspeakable challenges and a wealth of opportunities. For identity, my people were subjected to colonialism, exploitation, and injustice. For identity, I lost privileges and rights to childhood. For identity, I became a Lost Boy of Sudan. For identity, I incurred debt to acquire education to enable me to bring honor to my family by becoming a better seed of the nation.

While my journey has not ended, I am proud of what I have done and who I am. I am the son of Nyok Reech Akuok and Kuer Kur Dit. I am steadied by the words of my father and lifted by the song of my mother. I am cradled by the love of my wife and friends, old and new. I am a Dinka and an American. I have confronted death and embraced life, and I open my arms to the promises.

Acknowledgements

Someone once wrote on a bumper sticker "if you can read this, thank a teacher." I borrow a privilege to rewrite this phrase. If you find "DAYS OF REFUGEE" to be a good read, thank Sonya Cunningham, who in fact is a teacher.

I pay gratitude to my friend Sonya Cunningham for dedicating her initial editorial skills to enriching the quality and readability of this book.

Most importantly, it is gratifying to appreciate my wife and partner in this writing project, Yar Mayom Garang for giving me her timely contributions and encouragement in making my story available to the world.

Author Bio

Nathaniel Nyok is the founder and president of the Ambassadors for Change: The Nathaniel Chol Nyok Foundation—a not-for-profit organization dedicated to building a high school in South Sudan. Mr. Nyok, who is a diplomat, a humanitarian and a motivational speaker, holds a Bachelor's degree in International Affairs from Kennesaw State University in Atlanta, Georgia and a Master's degree in Diplomacy and International Relations from Seton Hall University in South Orange, New Jersey.

In 1987, at eight years old, the Sudan civil war separated Mr. Nyok and family. Mr. Nyok, along with a group of young boys, fled Sudan and trekked barefoot for thousands of miles to seek refuge in Ethiopia. During a journey that took about two months, Mr. Nyok encountered hunger, thirst, wild animals and crocodile-infested rivers. Becoming one of the Lost Boys of Sudan, Mr. Nyok registered as a refugee—living in two refugee camps in Ethiopia and Kenya for almost fifteen years before migrating to the United States in 2001.

A former legislative intern at the United States Senate with the Office of Senator Johnny Isakson (R-GA) and a former humanitarian and advocacy intern at Save the Children, Mr. Nyok is an activist on the Sudans, refugee rights, human rights and Africa in Washington, D.C.

www.ambassadorsforchange.org

CPSIA information can be obtained
at www.ICGtesting.com
Printed in the USA
BVHW030825020119
536864BV00001B/19/P